CONCILIUM

Theology in the Age of Renewal

CONCILIUM

Theology in the Age of Renewal

EDITORIAL DIRECTORS: Edward Schillebeeckx (Dogma) •
Herman Schmidt (Liturgy) • Alois Müller (Pastoral) •
Hans Küng (Ecumenism) • Franz Böckle (Moral Theology) •
Johannes B. Metz (Church and World) • Roger Aubert (Church
History) • ✠Néophytos Edelby and Teodoro Jiménez Urresti
(Canon Law) • Christian Duquoc (Spirituality) • Pierre Benoit and
Roland Murphy (Scripture)

CONSULTING EDITORS: Marie-Dominique Chenu • ✠Carlo
Colombo • Yves Congar • Andrew Greeley • Jorge Mejía •
Karl Rahner • Roberto Tucci

EXECUTIVE SECRETARY: (Awaiting new appointment),
Arksteestraat 3–5, Nijmegen, The Netherlands

Volume 57: Church History

EDITORIAL BOARD: Roger Aubert • Anton Weiler •
Giuseppe Alberigo • Quintin Aldea • J. Anastasiou •
François Bontinck • Victor Conzemius • Alphonse Dupront •
Enrique Dussel • John Tracy Ellis • Justo Fernandez-Alonso •
Jacques Gadille • Joseph Hajjar • James Hennesey • Erwin Iserloh •
Jerzy Kloczowski • M. David Knowles • Heinrich Lutz • James
Mackey • Henri Marrou • Giacomo Martina • Heiko Oberman •
Bernard Plongeron • Emile Poulat • Peter Manns • Peter
Stockmeier • José Tellechea • Brian Tierney • Hermann Tüchle

CHURCH HISTORY IN FUTURE PERSPECTIVE

Edited by
Roger Aubert

Herder and Herder

1970
HERDER AND HERDER
232 Madison Avenue, New York 10016

CONTENTS

PART III

DOCUMENTATION CONCILIUM

Editorial

SEVERAL reasons have led the editors of this issue of *Concilium* to devote it entirely to problems of method. It comes at a time when Church historians are tending more and more towards critical examination of their methods and even their aims.

Firstly, we have been aware of the attempts at renewal in the field of historical studies generally in the last few years. What is studied, the way in which it is done and the manner in which the findings of research are presented have all come under scrutiny. These attempts at renewal witness to a desire to discern the proper place of history and its relations with the other human sciences. Though the exact form such attempts take may vary according to the country and also according to major ideological differences, there is a general consensus of reaction against the positivism and historicism of preceding generations and a growing disenchantment with what has been termed "the history of events". What is now sought is a "global" history which, by employing the insights of sociology, psychology, cultural anthropology, human geography, and so on, highlights the cohesion and interdependence of the different factors involved: economic bases, social structures, political and ecclesiastical institutions, ideologies, scientific and technological developments, cultural manifestations. The first three articles try to outline a few of these fundamental trends and the bulletins in this issue attempt to make a preliminary assessment of two especially important aspects: the thinking behind the syntheses currently being elaborated and religious sociology's contribution to Church history.

Secondly, Church historians are confronted with the renewed and wider idea of the Church put forward by Vatican II. To begin with, the Church is the "people of God" and not merely the hierarchy: a notion which leads to greater emphasis being placed on the history of religious *life* and *mentality* than on the history of ecclesiastical institutions, dogmas and theology. Then, the hierarchy is not to be taken merely as the Pope and the Roman Curia acting through the bishops as intermediaries, but as the episcopal college in union with the See of Rome, which leads to increased emphasis on the original developments of the local Churches at the expense of the classic "history of the popes". Finally, the Roman Catholic Church's relationship to the other Christian Churches is seen in a new light suggesting that these should be included in an overall approach to "Church history", no longer simply because of their acts of dissent but because of the inner life of the communities they comprise which can claim in varying degrees to be part of Christ's Church. Professor Alberigo's article, basing itself on a series of concrete instances, calls for reflection on the change of heart needed, which is still in its earliest stages.

Thirdly, and more basically, Church historians feel challenged by the current, highly fruitful renewal in theology. Theology's concern to respond in the language of today to the questions posed by contemporary man has led many young theologians, who are reacting against the excesses of the historical theology so dear to their predecessors, to question the interest for the theologian of a study of the Church's past. Church history no longer automatically enjoys the privileged position freely accorded in the nineteenth century to any historical approach to a problem. For its own sake, therefore, it has to justify its usefulness, even its necessity, for the theological task as conceived in our day. Without claiming to have exhausted so vast a subject with so many ramifications, the two articles on Church history as a branch of theology and on the indispensable role of Church history for a correct interpretation of the sense and scope of the magisterium's pronouncements both help to guard against a certain type of exclusivism and certain naïvities. Bernard Plongeron's reflections widen our perspective by showing how religious history, renewed by contact with the other human sciences, can in turn help to renew theological education in the prevailing cultural environment.

May this issue increase awareness that the volume of *Concilium* reserved each year for Church history does not constitute a sudden aberration in an otherwise theological journal, but rather aims at reminding readers, through contact with concrete experience, of the proper aim of a balanced theology.

ROGER AUBERT
ANTON WEILER

PART I
ARTICLES

Anton Weiler

Church History and the Reorientation of the Scientific Study of History

I. Introduction

THERE has been a noticeable decline in the world of humane studies generally in interest in history—an interest which has for so long dominated this whole field. Far more attention is now given, for example, to theoretical and structurizing approaches to these disciplines and to empirical and quantifying methods. This is certainly also the case in the sphere of theology. In spite of continuing speculative interest in "historicity"[1] as an anthropological category, there are clearly good pastoral reasons for drawing the attention of theologians away from pure history. One of the principal reasons must be that the need to concentrate on the Church's tasks *here and now* has led to the growing conviction that the practice of constantly looking backwards at the Church's past produces very little in the way of material for pastoral preaching. Some Church historians have reacted to this objection by emphasizing more strongly the need to study the history, for example, of religiosity, the life of faith and the pastoral care of "ordinary" priests and believers. In responding in this way, however, they show that they are not really aware of the fact that the present "weariness of Church history"[2] has in fact far deeper roots. It is quite probable that the twentieth-century lack of feeling for history is attributable not only to the fact

[1] A. Darlapp, "Geschichtlichkeit", in *Lexikon für Theologie und Kirche,* 4 (1960), pp. 780–3.
[2] Joseph A. Fischer, "Kirchengeschichte heute", in *Theol.-prakt. Quartalschrift,* 112 (1964), p. 13.

that the rapid social changes of our own age have in fact broken our living bond with tradition, but also to a clear desire to overcome history. Instead of attempting once more to integrate history into the dynamic process of transformation that is taking place now on a world-wide scale and to ensure its continuity in this change, some people are opting for a "liberation from the historical consciousness" for the benefit of a rational society of rational men which will be brought about partly at least with the aid of the rationalized humane and social sciences. In a penetrating analysis, R. Wittram has recently made a number of observations which show clearly how great the distance has become between, for example, the comment of the younger Marx —"We recognize only one science, the science of history" (1845–1846)—and "man's dissociation from the sphere of history" nowadays, a phenomenon which has been acutely observed by the Swiss sociologist, Richard F. Behrendt, for example. Wittram has summarized his own conclusions as follows: "A shortening of the historical perspective to the post-revolutionary era, a protest against historical costume as an unintelligible value, a break in continuity by repression or national guilt and a silent displacement of speech so that it has become intelligible, but lacking in any historical dimension."[3]

Liberation from and the banishment of the historical consciousness seems to many people to open the way for history itself, the history of the future. Man's feeling with regard to the history of the Church is rooted in this attitude towards history as such. The twentieth-century situation seems to very many people to be so essentially different from the phases that preceded it that certain "critical" Catholics feel the need to work out a completely new design of "Church" and preferably without reference to the tiresome burden of history. And, just as secular language is becoming a-historical and functional, as a means of making plans for the future operational, so too are certain theologians tempted to make

---

[3] R. Wittram, *Anspruch und Fragwürdigkeit der Geschichte. Sechs Vorlesungen zur Methodik der Geschichtswissenschaft und zur Ortsbestimmung der Historie* (Göttingen, 1969) (*Kleine Vandenhoeck-Reihe*, 297/298/299), p. 18. The text from Marx, quoted on p. 23, is from *Die deutsche Ideologie*, I, published in *Die Frühschriften*, ed. S. Landshut (1953), p. 346; the text from R. F. Behrendt, quoted on p. 8, is from *Der Mensch im Licht der Soziologie* (Stuttgart, 1963²), p. 68.

new statements about the "Church" which, compared with earlier statements, often give the distinct impression of having lost all continuity with the past.

All the same, simply to describe the present lack of feeling for history is not to give a full account of the twentieth-century attitude towards history. Not all those who aim to renew society and the Church want to work in a vacuum of this kind. There are also those people who believe that what is necessary is a new attitude towards history which is above all *positive*, especially if this is to form the basis of the new critical way of thinking about society and the Church. Critical commitment to the building up of a new world and a new Church leads to a reorientation of the scientific study of history.

The historian is therefore placed between two fires. Attempts to dissociate himself from history on the one hand and attempts to put history at the service of the present and of a new future on the other hand contrast so strongly with the traditional view of the historian that it is no exaggeration to say that there is a serious conflict. So far, a solution to this crisis that is acceptable to everyone has not been found.

In this article, I should like to consider the problems that confront the historian in the light of the demands made by man's commitment to the task of renewing society and the Church here and now and especially where the consequences for the science of Church history are concerned. The problems which arise from the idea of the lack of feeling for history today will not be considered here.

The conflict that arises from the first-mentioned series of demands is not entirely new to the Church historian. He was faced with a similar crisis in the earlier controversy about the relationship between theology and Church history. One of the authorities in this sphere, H. Jedin, has summarized his views on this question in an article in a well-known lexicon,[4] which at the same time includes all the relevant books and articles up to 1960. A

---

[4] "Kirchengeschichte", in *Lexikon für Theologie und Kirche*, 6 (1961), pp. 209-18, with bibliography; foreword in *Handbuch der Kirchengeschichte*; "Kirchengeschichte" by G. Denzler, in *Was ist Theologie*, ed. by E. Neuhäusler, E. Gössmann (Munich, 1966), pp. 138-68; see also bulletins in this number.

central point in this debate was the division between faith and theology on the one hand and Church history as a specialized scientific study on the other. In this conflict, the concepts of faith, theology and science were subject to a change of emphasis under the influence of existentialist ideas. This debate has, in my opinion, not yet produced many tangible results. It is probably better, then, to approach the problem, not from the point of view of theology, but rather from the point of view of the study of history in general. The first general question is therefore—what is the scientific study of history and what are its aims?

II. WHAT IS THE SCIENTIFIC STUDY OF HISTORY AND HOW SHOULD THE CHURCH HISTORIAN USE IT?

Let us first try to define briefly what the study of history is according to present-day views, that is, according to the views of historians who work along the lines determined by present-day scientific theories and not by those of the nineteenth century. Despite the fact that there are so many schools of philosophy now, it could be said fairly safely that philosophers and theoreticians generally speaking attach a great deal of value to reflection about the irreducible pre-scientific environment in which man is closely associated with his world, and that philosophy and scientific theory have, so to speak, the task of interpreting and throwing light on this pre-scientific introduction, with every conscious or unconscious human capacity for perception in the world to an understanding of this very irreducibility in man and his association with the world. It is to this pre-scientifically given and not always reflectively experienced pattern of forces, within which man is or should be a nodal point, that the forces of the past from which man has arisen in history belong. Man's state of being in history must be illuminated and he must come to an understanding of this state in the light of history. It is this demand which determines the investigations made by the science of history and the results of historical study must contribute to man's understanding of himself and his being in history *now*.

On the subject of Church history, Jedin has said, following Erich Benz:[5] "With the help of the scientific historical method,

---

[5] *Kirchengeschichte in ökumenischer Sicht* (Leiden and Cologne, 1961).

the history of the Church moves forward from an unreflective being in the Church to a conscious grasp of the Church as an historical factor. This development of Church history is as dependent on the Church's understanding of herself as it is on the elaboration and refinement of historical criticism which makes use, for example, of the study of original sources, bibliography and all available auxiliary sciences".[6]

We may therefore draw two conclusions from this. Firstly, the scientific study of Church history ought in fact to be carried out like any branch of profane history, in other words, the scholar working in this sphere should not be slow to tread new paths if these are being followed by those who specialize in the science of profane history. I shall discuss this question first, in the following, that is, the third section of this article. My second conclusion is, however, even more important, namely that a different understanding of the Church produces a differently orientated Church history. This different understanding can be brought about, for example, by a different understanding of society, of which the Church forms a part. Both these points are very closely related. I shall deal with the second in the fourth section of this article.

III. The Renewal of Historical Methods in the Light of the Social Sciences

In his work, the Church historian uses not only the traditional historical methods that have developed since the seventeenth century, but also, increasingly, the more recent methods.[7] Let me give an example of this.

Both the older and the new methods are found side by side at the level of medieval Church history. Two types of historian are met with in this sphere of study. The first uses the so-called auxiliary sciences of historical research in the pursuit of his object. He is, for example, aided by palaeography or the study of ancient handwriting, diplomatology or the science of charters, decrees and so on, which provide him with the criteria which he needs

---

[6] Jedin, "Kirchengeschichte", op. cit., p. 211.
[7] See O. Brunner, Neue Wege der Verfassungs- und Sozialgeschichte (Göttingen, 1968[2]), p. 12. See also the article by C. W. Mönnich, below, p. 42.

to judge whether traditional documents of a juridical nature are authentic or not, and codicology or the archaeology of manuscripts. He can therefore make use of philological and other critical methods of this kind to help him to present his sources in as pure a form as possible for interpretation. Criticism of the sources also plays a part in the editing and publishing of texts provided with a scholarly array of footnotes concerning textual variants, so that it is possible for any trained reader to judge for himself whether the text that is presented is authentic. All of this work can, moreover, be ultimately traced back to the humanists and Church historians of the Renaissance and baroque periods, who tried to purify their precious texts inherited from classical antiquity and the early Church of their medieval deposits.

The second type of historian also applies these methods to his work or at least gratefully accepts the results that his colleagues have achieved in providing reliable texts by these methods, but his research goes further and deeper. He is more concerned with exploring the inner structure of the Church in its different ethnological, geographical and chronological units and the Church's corresponding understanding of herself. In this work, he takes into account the methods used by the social sciences and he makes as much use as possible of types and models as his analysis of the material produced by the philological and critical methods enables him to do. He establishes hypotheses for interpretation and tests these against the "facts". In this way, he tries to form an interconnection between the pluriform historical data that he finds in the field that he is investigating so that he can obtain an overall view of the whole of society during the different medieval periods and thus ascertain which factors brought about the lasting link between individuals or groups at that time or, on the contrary, led to its change and collapse. A combination of Church history and secular history in its institutional, social and economic aspects is particularly well suited to this purpose. He will study the different elements of society separately in order to bring them together in a more or less coherent outline of the inner structure. Finally, he will consider the history of ideas in the period in order to understand the intellectual life of the Middle Ages, which came about as the result of interaction between Christian,

Jewish, Greek, Roman, Byzantine and Germanic ideas. A society is made stable by a coherent legitimation—it is the idea which sustains a social group or a period, through which constant adhesion to the group structurized in this way is determined and stimulated.[8] (I do not wish, of course, to claim that religion, in the sense of a consistent theory, has to be understood as reflecting social relationships. As Wittram has correctly observed, that would be an analytical error.[9])

This process of stabilization had advanced a long way in the Middle Ages and the Church was entirely involved in this movement towards stabilization. Research into the history of the medieval Church has the task of clarifying, for example, the various ways in which the Church became thus involved by assimilation. To begin with, this research often has to confine itself to regional analysis, since it is sometimes only along this path that a more general structural investigation in a wider context is possible.[10]

Within the framework of a large-scale structural analysis of the whole of the Middle Ages, then, it is possible to determine how the Church realized and understood herself in each of the periods constituting the Middle Ages. I should like, in this context, to quote two standard formulas, the first seeing the Church "as the entelechy of the Western Christian community of peoples (700–1300)"[11] and the second commenting on the Gregorian reforms: "the most decisive break-through of a Roman Catholic character in history".[12] Both of these formulas show the extent to which the Church and medieval Christianity were,

---

[8] See L. Laeyendecker, "A Sociological Approach to Secularization", in *Concilium* (September 1969), pp. 6–10 (American edn., vol. 47); for this model, the author refers to P. Berger and T. Luckmann, *The Social Construction of Reality* (New York, 1967²).

[9] R. Wittram, *op. cit.*, p. 90, referring to P. Bollhagen, *Einführung in das Stadium der Geschichte* (East Berlin, 1966), p. 61.

[10] For a later period, see, for example, M. Cloet's lengthy study, *Het kerkelijk leven in een landelijke dekenij van Vlaanderen tijdens de XVIIe eeuw. Tielt van 1609 tot 1700* (Louvain, 1968). In his introduction, the author indicates the historical framework of the whole Church within which this detailed study of religious life of the rural population of Flanders should be situated.

[11] H. Jedin, "Kirchengeschichte", *op. cit.*, p. 125.

[12] F. Kempf, "Gregorianische Reform", in *Lexikon für Theologie und Kirche*, 4 (1960), p. 1196.

according to these authors, an extension of each other and completely absorbed each other so that they were one single reality.

IV. THE CHANGING PERSPECTIVE OF (CHURCH) HISTORY

As I have already said, at the end of section II, it is far more important that the Church's changing understanding of herself can undoubtedly lead to a changed perspective of Church history. The Church's changing understanding of herself in the present century has clearly been at least partly influenced by the social changes of the twentieth century, which are always manifested much more noticeably.[13] The latter have given rise to a different attitude with regard to history, as I mentioned earlier on. If we look back at the period of the "new" history, at least two factors have, according to Otto Brunner,[14] contributed towards the breakthrough of the earlier idea of the cohesion of European history within which, for example, the Reformation and the Counter-Reformation made their appearance. The first is the political and social change that has taken place since the end of the eighteenth century, a change that has been called "fundamental democratization" by Karl Mannheim or the "transition towards industrial and bureaucratic society". Secondly, this structural change has sometimes been interpreted, for example, by Werner Conze, as the "European revolution". This term clearly indicates that the radical change that has taken place originated in Europe and has spread from Europe to the rest of the world. Brunner goes on to say, in this context, that the task of the modern historian is therefore to learn how to distinguish the basic tendencies which have led to this recent revolution which was, in the first place, confined to Europe, but has, in the twentieth century, embraced the whole world.[15]

This changing perspective which presents itself to the "secular" historian from a changed present with a changed view of the future must also concern the Church historian. In a place that is rather hidden from the public that is interested in theology,

[13] See O. Köhler, "Probleme des Kulturwandels im 20. Jahrhundert", *Saeculum*, 14 (1963), pp. 60–81.
[14] O. Brunner, *op. cit.*, pp. 12–13.
[15] O. Brunner, *op. cit.*, p. 14.

Francis X. Murphy[16] has pleaded that Church history should be orientated in the same direction as "secular" history. As he correctly points out, not only the new universalistic historical and sociological methods of such scholars as Toynbee, Valery and Sorokin, but also the changes that have taken place in man's view of the world in the twentieth century, have led to the gradual eclipse of the study and writing of history in the manner of Ranke. The historian has, Murphy claims, to give his attention now to the *whole* course of human history "in an attempt to limn the perspective of the whole of man's development".[17] In the present number of *Concilium*, C. W. Mönnich also includes the future in his speculations about Church history.

V. NORMALIZED HISTORIOGRAPHY?

It is possible to say that the new situation of the twentieth century has accentuated concern for the present and the future not only on the part of the contemporary historian, but also on the part of historians of every kind. No one will have much trouble with views expressed in this way about the orientation of secular and Church history towards the future. Orientation towards the future is an existential experience which has recently become conscious and which is being eagerly cultivated. The future does not, however, simply come about of its own accord—it has to be made by men. What, then, will this human future be like? Is it not a question of free choice and therefore subjective? From where do we derive our norms for future activity? What are the ethics that should guide us here? Should they be subjective ethics or is there such a thing as objective ethics? These questions directly concern the historian who is trying to orientate his work towards the future. In considering the answers that have been given to these questions, we are confronted with very many thorny problems, many of which go to the very heart of contemporary difficulties.

We have learnt from the existential philosophy of Heidegger and from the theories of, for example, Aron, Marrou, Romein

---

[16] F. X. Murphy, "History and the Catholic Historian", in *The Irish Ecclesiastical Record*, 89 (1958), pp. 412–23, 90 (1958), pp. 89–103, 92 (1959), pp. 73–89 and 151–69.   [17] F. X. Murphy, *op. cit.*, 89, p. 418.

and Collingwood that it is not only impossible, but also undesirable to eliminate subjectivity entirely from our interpretation of history.[18] Readers of *Concilium* can be regarded as being informed of the modern view of hermeneutics as the method employed nowadays in the scientific study of the humanities generally and of history in particular. We should not be surprised, then, if the practical consequences for historiography are now being drawn from these theoretical ideas, with all the dangers that are involved in them. Murphy, for example, acknowledges that we are, in one respect, living in a "post-Christian era",[19] but he insists that the Church historian has the task of keeping the memory alive in men's minds of the Church's achievements in the past and her heritage, but that he must do this in the light of his firm conviction and faith and always *with the demands of the future in mind*. The Church historian, Murphy believes, has, by virtue of his knowledge of the Church and his faith in her universal task, to help modern man to prepare for the implications of the "one world" which confronts him now. Faith and the interpretation of the future are therefore the norms for the Church historian. Murphy quotes the words of Pius XII[20] spoken at the Tenth International Historical Congress at Rome on 7 September 1955. According to Pius XII, the task of the Church historian is to contribute to the religious and moral commitment of the Church with the unity of the world in mind. This means writing Church history (again, if necessary) in the light of the future, which has to be made, in part, by the Church and with the help of faith.

Some historians will undoubtedly feel a certain resistance to this kind of normalization. They will agree with the closing words of Pius XII's above-mentioned address because they too believe that it is the historian's task to strive towards objectivity, impartiality and complete absence of prejudice. What the Pope said on this occasion was: "May science, in its pursuit of truth,

[18] See A. G. Weiler, "Geschiedenis en hermeneutiek. Schets van enige theoretische grondlijnen van de geschiedeniswetenschap als interpretatieve wetenschap", in *Interpretatieleer. Annalen Thijmgenootschap*, 57 (1969), pp. 57–112.

[19] F. X. Murphy, *op. cit.*, 90 (1958), p. 91.

[20] Text in, for example, *Ecclesia docens*, June–October 1955, Hilversum (1958).

not be influenced by subjective considerations". Is this expectation of the future not a subjective speculation, then?"

Those who object to the link between faith and the scientific study of history can immediately produce examples of how this study has been and, in certain cases, still is linked to the furtherance of a particular ideology which is offensive and unacceptable. Although it is to some extent already fading from living memory, one example from the European past springs to mind readily enough—the use of history in the struggle against the terms of the treaty of Versailles and its further distortion by the National Socialist movement in Germany. The present situation in Europe provides even more striking examples of the manipulation of the science of history—in the German Democratic Republic and the Soviet Union, historians have the primary task of helping to fashion a Communist consciousness, a Communist morality and a Communist society. In a word, their first duty is the formation of the new man of the society of the future.[21] A. Dalling[22] may, of course, speak of Clio as the concubine of the Soviet Union and Walter Hofer[23] may call her the mistress of the ruling totalitarian party, but for the Communist world the bourgeois historians of the West are the lackeys of imperialism. There do seem to be many objections to "committed" historiography. Many Western historians do not, therefore, want history to act as a *magistra vitae* and prefer to scorn all commitment and fulfil a rather dry as dust function in the world. This attitude is, however, being criticized more and more at present. It is a criticism which must be taken seriously.

It is, after all, not only in the Soviet Union that attempts are being made to transcend the liberal idea of history. Even in America, there has been a noticeable reaction against the kind

[21] K. Marko, *Sowjethistoriker zwischen Ideologie und Wissenschaft. Aspekte der sowjetrussischen Wissenschaftspolitik seit Stalins Tod, 1953–1963* (Institut für Sowjetologie, Fasc. 7 (Cologne, 1964), p. 11; see also A. P. Mendel, "Current Soviet Theory of History. New Trends or Old?", in *The American Historical Review*, 72 (1967), pp. 50–73.

[22] A. Dalling, "The Soviet Social Sciences after Stalin", in *Iron Curtains in Scholarship. The Exchange of Knowledge in a Divided World*, ed. Howard W. Winger (Chicago, 1958), p. 86; quoted by Marko, p. 22.

[23] W. Hofer, "Geschichtsschreibung als Instrument totalitärer Politik", in *Neue Zürcher Zeitung*, 17 (18 January 1964), p. 11; quoted by Marko, p. 22.

of historiography which takes the liberal American consensus of opinion as its starting-point. There is a growing movement in sociology, economics, political science and history in the United States, that of the so-called "New Left", which is opposed to the political conservatism of the older generation, history "at the service of an élitist and aristocratic definition of society and the American celebration",[24] the power of the traditional historians at the universities and their thinking which is conditioned by the "establishment", and the failure of these historians to provide a "usable past"[25] which can give direction to the desire and plans of the younger generation for a radically new community. This "New Left" movement is therefore calling for a new understanding of history which can be used as a political weapon in the service, however, of the new community.

How have American Church historians reacted to this? They certainly seem to be far removed from Acton's claim that Church history should make moral judgments about the past with the preservation of the Church's identity as the Church of Jesus Christ in mind.[26] According to an analysis provided by John F. Dolan,[27] the weakness that is discernible in present-day American Catholic Church historiography is the tendency to omit any interpretation of the facts and to continue to work along the lines of Ranke. He gives only one exception to the general rule of "a maximum of quotations from the sources and a minimum of interpretation" and that is a single study by Thomas McAvoy.[28] And how does American Protestant historiography operate? For a long time, this has been characterized by the production of de-

---

[24] I. Unger, "The 'New Left' and American History. Some Recent Trends in United States Historiography", in *The American Historical Review*, 72 (1966–67), pp. 1237–63.

[25] H. S. Commager, *The Search for a Usable Past, and Other Essays in Historiography* (New York, 1967).

[26] H. S. Commager, "Should the Historian Sit in Judgment?", *op. cit.*, pp. 300–22.

[27] J. F. Dolan, "Changing Trends in Anglo-American Church History. A Survey", in *Reformata Reformanda. Festgabe für H. Jedin*, II (Münster, 1965), pp. 558–94. The passage to which I refer will be found on p. 576.

[28] Dolan refers to several studies by McAvoy concerning "the formation of the Catholic minority in the United States", *op. cit.*, p. 585; similarly, McAvoy's article "Americanism: The Myth and the Reality", in *Concilium* (September 1967), pp. 60–66 (American edn., Vol. 27) certainly deserves to be mentioned.

tailed studies without any reference to the world of today, without any attempt to interpret or to take up a position and without any indication that the author is writing as a member of a Church community. The attacks made by Beard, Becker and Turner,[29] who have produced a "pragmatic revolt" in American historiography, against this so-called scientific writing of history have introduced new scientific methods from other disciplines into historical studies and have opened the eyes of Church historians to the non-theological factors which influence the form and direction of the history of the Church. Despite this, however, the positivistic idea of historiography still predominates to a very great extent in these new methods. Dolan, on the other hand, has argued that, ever since the nineteen-thirties, there has been a growing awareness of the inadequacy of sociological analysis, for example, to provide hypotheses which can give us a better understanding of Church history. Interest has been shifting towards the ideological and theological interpretation of the history of the Church—an interpretation which has sometimes been called "ideational"—in which not only the neutral questions about *how* and *why* the Church has developed historically are studied, but also the *content* of this process of historical development is constantly verified.[30]

The situation in America is not an isolated phenomenon. In Germany too, there has been a wide-ranging discussion about the "foundations" of Church history, a discussion which has to be situated within the wider framework of what is known as the "crisis of the foundations of the scientific study of history".[31] The validity of the positivistic idea and the psychological understanding of the contents of history are being questioned there as well and especially in the sphere of Church history. Since it is becoming more and more obvious that "it is impossible fully to understand the contents of revelation rationally, an independent

[29] For these men who are attempting to renew American historiography, see, for example, C. Strout, *The Pragmatic Revolt in American History: Carl Becker and Charles Beard* (New Haven, 1958).

[30] J. F. Dolan, "Changing Trends", *op. cit.*, p. 591.

[31] See, for example, O. F. Anderle, "Die Geschichtswissenschaft in der Krise", in *Festgabe Joseph Lortz*, II (Baden-Baden, 1958), pp. 491-550; E. Pitz, "Geschichtliche Strukturen. Betrachtungen zur angeblichen Grundlagenkrise der Geschichtswissenschaft", in *Historische Zeitschrift*, 198 (1964), pp. 265-305.

religious category of knowledge has therefore to be evolved", as Fritz Wagner has correctly observed.[32] The tendency therefore is to reject a purely rational understanding of Church history and to develop a *theological* method, rather than a strictly historical method for interpreting the historical and anthropological situation. The most difficult problem, however, in this new approach is undoubtedly how to reveal the religious meaning that is present in the individual event. The theological hermeneutics which provide the guide-lines for this method have, according to some scholars, a fundamentally *normative* part to play here.

Even "secular" historians in Germany are at one with their colleagues in the field of political science in opposing the "anti-normative" or "unpolitical" element in the German tradition of writing history,[33] which is subject to the same criticism, although here of course applied to the situation in Germany, as the American form of historiography with its emphasis on the "establishment". The argument is that anyone who claims to write history that is "free of values" is implicitly acknowledging the value of wanting to be free of values, in other words, he is admitting that his thinking is liberal and positivistic and that he himself is not free of values. The great champions of the new political science are Arnold Brecht, Leo Strauss and Eric Voegelin[34] and they have clearly enough been joined by "pure" historians such as Karl Bracher.[35] M. Brands[36] discusses in his book the choice be-

[32] F. Wagner, "Zweierlei Mass der Geschichtsschreibung—eine offene Frage", in *Saeculum*, 10 (1959), p. 114.

[33] See M. Brands, *Historisme als ideologie. Het "onpolitieke" en "anti-normatieve" element in de Duitse geschiedwetenschap* (Assen, 1965); this book has a summary in German.

[34] For a list of books and articles by and about Brecht and Strauss, see Brands, *Historisme als ideologie, op. cit.*, pp. 262 and 273-4; by and about E. Voegelin, including a (critical) discussion of several of his works, see L. Freund, "Einige Reflexionen über das Wesen der geistes- und sozialwissenschaftlichen Erkenntnisvorgänge", in *Recht im Dienste der Menschenwürde, Festschrift für H. Kraus* (Würzburg, 1964), pp. 489-518, in which Brecht's theory is also discussed.

[35] For a list of books and articles by and about Bracher, see Brands, *Historisme als ideologie, op. cit.*, pp. 261-2; a reprint of Bracher's most important articles will be found in *Deutschland zwischen Demokratie und Diktatur. Beiträge zur neueren Politik* (Berne, 1964).

[36] *Op. cit.*, p. 250; in connection with Church history, see P. Meinhold's article, "Geschichtskritik und Kirchenerneuerung", in *Saeculum*, 9 (1958), pp. 1-21.

tween a conformist approach and a critical ideal. Transcendental thinking and thinking in terms of natural law are given a new function through the formulation of criteria concerning the *correctness* of the political choice, the correctness of the commitment that is demanded of everyone in private and in public life. The ethical question and the normative answer to this question—an answer which is transcendentally conditioned—are given the most explicit emphasis in all scientific study, including that of history.

If this is really the case, why should the Church historian, who has, in his *faith*, an image of the *future* which is theologically based, not, in accordance with his commitment to his faith, practise his scientific study of history for the benefit of that future, *ut omnes unum sint?* It would seem to be an obvious conclusion that, wherever the subjectivity of the historian is theoretically recognized, nothing should prevent the Catholic historian from writing history in the light of his faith.

VI. Some Critical Notes on the Above

There are, however, still a number of questions which have to be discussed in greater detail. One characteristic which is common to all the views which are expressed above is their orientation towards the future. However attractive these ideas may seem at first sight, there are certainly theoretical and practical objections which can be made against them and these objections have nothing whatever to do with conservative ideas or with a liberal practice which prides itself on being "free of values". There can be no doubt that "future" is a category of human, historical time. Without consciousness of the past, man cannot acquire any consciousness of time—there is no future without history.[37] Human consciousness is the constantly actual, present place where both categories coincide. As theoreticians of the science of history such as R. Wittram and hermeneutists such as E. Betti[38] have correctly pointed out, however, the question about the past arises in man's

[37] K. D. Erdmann, "Die Zukunft als Kategorie der Geschichte", in *Historische Zeitschrift*, 198 (1964), pp. 44–90; R. Wittram, "Anspruch und Fragwürdigkeit der Geschichte", *op. cit.*, p. 97.

[38] *Die Hermeneutik als allgemeine Methodik der Geisteswissenschaften* (Tübingen, 1962) (Philosophie und Geschichte 78/79).

present consciousness of the contemporary situation, but this question must afterwards "be held captive and modified by the independent strangeness of the past".[39] There cannot, in this case, be a catalogue of questions which are voluntarily and ideologically determined, to which the answer is known in advance and into which the only research that is approved is that which is accepted in advance as "pregnant for the future". Scientific historical research and the scientific writing of (Church) history should not be debased to the level of a denial of established principles which correctly require the historian, when he enters the past, to "measure the proportions of history not in accordance with their relationship with the present, but in accordance with how they have been determined by their period".[40] This is not required by the historical method. It is rather an anthropological demand with regard to the *object* which has to be honoured if the "anthropology to which the historian adheres is to qualify his understanding of history",[41] is to be accepted as valid for the interpreting *subject*. The dogmatic attempt to establish one single view of man and one single scale of values which will be the criterion for all judgment and all action is a fanatical effort to overcome history itself by the force of reason and the determination of the human will. But the conquest of history in this way destroys man because he is forced into a life in accordance with his "nature", in other words, the direction which his life is expected to take is given to him, not in accordance with the pluriformity of historical development, but unequivocally and in accordance with natural law. This may even, in extreme cases, lead to a totalitarian exclusion of the human free will and the possibility of free choice and eventually even to a period in history when men will be manipulated as "products of human engineering", will follow, without any will of their own, the ideals that are put before them, will react as required in a stereotyped manner to conditioned and unconditioned signals as though they were hypnotized and will only think the thoughts that they are allowed to think.

The struggle against anti-normative historicism has been raging

[39] R. Wittram, "Anspruch und Fragwürdigkeit der Geschichte", *op. cit.*, p. 16.
[40] *Ibid*.   [41] *Ibid*.

ever since the First World War with the same degree of commitment as now. It is therefore not difficult to understand that the destruction of the sense of history in Germany which resulted from this struggle left the way free for the "political masters of the compulsory ideologies of the future rise of the nation",[42] a way which eventually led, after the Second World War, to that basic lack of feeling for history which makes the scientific study of history degenerate so easily into applied sociology. Karel Kupisch has indicated the change of method which went together with this process: "Because it is too complicated, the historical method is transformed into cybernetics and the computor replaces the rational mind." Dissatisfaction with the liberal bourgeois philosophy and with the political impotence brought about by this attitude led to a Nietzschean attack on the past which was supported by a suprahistorical consciousness. Kupisch, a German himself, has said of his own people that "they made the same tragic mistake that so many Germans have made—they believed that they only had to possess the 'right' philosophy in order to be able to put the life of the mind in order".[43]

This dissatisfaction seems to have returned again. There is a great deal of opposition everywhere to the liberal idea of science, attempts are being made to strengthen the ethical consciousness and a search is being made for a new formula for a healthy society. Theology, long ago dethroned as queen of the sciences by the process of radical secularization that has been taking place, is now becoming a "political" theology alongside other political sciences. The science of history—even that of Church history— is also being called upon to exercise a normative function of criticizing society.

There is, however, no simple criterion for the choice between (neo-) dogmatism and (neo-) liberalism—both claim to champion the dignity of man and both aim to save him from the destruction that is threatening from the other side. Every historian has to decide for himself which approach is the better guarantee of human dignity and which attitude he will therefore adopt. But scientific thinking in history as such also has to be guaranteed on

<hr>

[42] K. Kupisch, "Wider die Achtung der Geschichte", *Wider die Achtung der Geschichte. Festschrift Hans-Joachim Schoeps* (Munich, 1969), p. 108.
[43] *Ibid.*, p. 113.

the left and on the right, if they are really to command the commitment of the historian himself. The same also applies to any similar field of study—political science, political theology and critical sociology as well as the critical science of secular or Church history. None of these disciplines can escape from the demand of scientific thinking, which is, of course, quite different from ethical conviction.[44]

What is basic to all these ideas, however, is that the *essence* of man is *not* known *in advance* in the study of history, but that this has first to be given to us via the situation of being man in history. In the pluriformity of anthropologies today, there is undoubtedly a common pre-scientific desire to know what man's being ought to be and a measure of agreement is certainly possible between thinkers who differ radically if this is formulated negatively, in other words, what being man ought *not* to be. Man is not, however, given more than this transcendental orientation unless he is prepared, in faith, to follow those authoritative words which define his being positively and in which his transcendental orientation is reflected. In any case, it is undoubtedly the future that will reveal to man what he is, a being which is given to him and, although he does not have it at his own disposal, always comes towards him.

I believe therefore that Church history also operates as a scientific study at the same level of illuminating the understanding of history. The difference here is, however, that the essence of what the Church is *is* given at the outset. We have the original texts which tell us what Jesus and his first followers said and how he and they understood themselves as borne up by the "words of eternal life". Historical criticism can operate here with, for example, the texts of Luke, who was himself the first "Church historian", but it cannot get rid of the fact of Luke's faith in the Lord and his universal mission, nor can it, in whatever way it may be exercised, in the study of Church history, prevent believers from following Luke's faith themselves.

The being of the Church has, however, not been recorded univocally and unambiguously in the words of these texts. Here too, we have been given a pre-scientific orientation in faith which has

44 See K. Jaspers, *Die Idee der Universität* (Heidelberg, 1961), pp. 41-2.

to be made explicit in constantly different ways with the passage of time. In doing this, however, we shall never be able to disregard the first Christian community, the first documents, the first witnesses, the first centuries and the first councils, in which testimony was borne, in close proximity to the Lord, to the way in which Christians thought, at the very beginning, the Church ought to be.

VII. CONCLUSION

Church history does not automatically produce a suprahistorical view of the supra-historical theological essence and being of the Church. The view of the Church provided by Church history changes with history itself. Revelation and history can perhaps be made to harmonize with each other from the point of view of historical *theology* as long as this way of thinking is socially acceptable, as it was from the time of Augustine to that of Bossuet. Round about 1800, however, there was a dividing line, usually marked by Hegel, between the normative and absolutist period and the historical and relativistic period.[45] Since the rise of historicism, thinkers have been confronted not only with the problem of the *nature* and *being* or *essence* of things, but also with that of their *history*.

These two principles can only be reconciled by allowing the value of each to be seen within the framework of a universal anthropological theory, and faith has an irreplaceable function in the preparation of this theory. It teaches that the "community of man" is predestined to be the "community of salvation" and acknowledges that it is God's will that all men should achieve this salvation through acknowledging his Son Jesus Christ. But none of us has the right to ideologize his own insight into the Gospel and his own faith to such an extent that he begins to write "critical Church history" in the sense that he regards it as his task, on the basis of a "decision of the kind made by a normative theological control commission", to bring about the "radical critical destruction of everything that has come between us and Christ in the course of history".[46] None of this can be scientifically established.

[45] K. Kupisch, "Wider die Ächtung der Geschichte", *op. cit.*, p. 119.
[46] *Ibid.*, p. 123.

There would, then, seem to be only two extremes—normative absolutism or an historical relativism without norms. The distinctive character of the scientific study of history is, however, denied in both extremes. This study, including that of Church history, is an interpretative science. Every historian knows that his ultimate task is to interpret the results of research into sources and that, in carrying out this task, he must not hide behind a computor, but must have the courage to offer *his* understanding of history and *his* interpretation as a meaningful relationship of facts that has been produced by *his* mental activity to his colleagues and to the world. If his work satisfies the demands of the scientific method and of logical analysis, then the ensuing debate can concern itself with the *correctness* of the points of departure. This discussion will, however, be—ultimately and perhaps at a very late hour—not a scientific dialogue, but rather a conversation between seeking people, each of whom has chosen his own anthropology (some of them will have chosen the Christian view of man), but each of whom will be ready to discuss, quite openly, the other's presuppositions and unconscious desires, in the hope that light will be shed on their common problems. Doctrinaire intolerance does not produce any light of this kind, but as long as we face history with open questions, we shall be acting as living people who reject the domination of both extremes of scientific ideology. The Church historian should remain open to what the community of Jesus Christ can be, but it is only if he does not let himself be bound in advance to any established opinion in his own historical investigations that some light may perhaps be thrown for him, in this open investigation of different realizations on the fringe of his scientific work, on what the Church has been and can be.

Translated by David Smith

John Cobb

Towards a Displacement
of Historicism and Positivism

In modern Western man there have arisen two forms of consciousness that have striven with each other and with traditional and religious forms. These are the scientific consciousness and the historical consciousness.

The scientific consciousness is the objectifying consciousness. It objectifies in two senses. First, it separates the object from the perceiver, recognizing the object's differentness and autonomy, and allowing the object to be itself and to display its own properties rather than grasping it in terms of its usefulness and meaning to the perceiver. This mode of consciousness allows the object to shape the categories by which it is interpreted rather than imposing the perceiver's pre-existing categories upon the object. Second, the scientific consciousness objectifies also in the sense of denuding its object of all subjectivity. The object is viewed as being only that which it gives itself to be when apprehended by the perceiver. No being in itself or for itself is acknowledged. Even when the object of investigation is a human being, the scientific consciousness brackets and ignores the subjectivity of its object.

The first mode of objectification, which is open to the object in its particularity and allows a realistic perception of the object, is finally vitiated by the second. This second mode of objectification denudes the object of all that can give it being over against the perceiver. The object is what it is for the perceiver and nothing more. It is allowed to answer only the questions asked by the scientist: no answers are imposed upon it. Since such questions are about universals rather than particulars, the object is reduced to an instance of a general category or law. Since the questions that follow are about the relations of universals to each other rather than about the inter-relations of the instances, the scientific consciousness moves more and more into the sphere of forms and their logical relations and leaves behind the sphere of particulars and their causal relations.

In the end the scientific consciousness retains only the most tenuous contact with the concrete objects of its initial investigation. Its formalizations know time only as a symbol that is reversible or even replaceable. Questions of meaning, value, being and existence no longer arise, except in so far as the questioning itself can be viewed as an object for investigation. Finally, scientific knowing in its turn must be made an object of scientific investigation and thus be denuded of its character of knowing.

To some extent the historical consciousness shares with the scientific consciousness its view of nature. Nature is seen as mere object—mere instantiation of general propositions for which time is inessential. The reality of nature is supposed to reside in its apprehension in human experience. For the historical consciousness, human experience is the bearer of all reality.

Human experience as known by the historical consciousness is incurably temporal and incurably particular. The particular must be understood in terms of how it came about and what it contributed towards, rather than as an instance of something more general. Furthermore, the objects of the historian's study cannot be denied their subjectivity. They embody purposes, meanings, values, thought, feeling and vision. What occurs interests the historian as somehow arising from or contributing to the subjective life of man.

The historical consciousness is ambivalent as to the employment of the first mode of scientific objectivity. The possibility of achieving in the study of the human the degree of neutrality the scientist attains in studying nature is questioned. But possibility is not the crucial issue, since perfect realization is not necessary to the efficacy of an ideal. Neutrality is only partly achieved in the natural sciences, but the effort to attain it has been fundamental to their progress. The important question is desirability.

If the historian strives for this type of neutrality, the result can only be a complete relativism of values. He can present every human norm and ideal as factually real and as a function of the history in which it arose. His own ideals and those of his contemporaries must appear equally as products of the historical process. If there are currently conflicting ideals, each must appear as equally a part of the historical process. The belief that some norms are *really* worthy of obedience and that some ideals are *really* worthy of realization is dissipated in a nihilistic relativism. The historian's own ideal of objectivity and neutrality does not escape the encompassing relativism.

Since the justification of objectivity is undercut by objectivity, the historian sometimes adopts another alternative. He exists and writes at a particular moment. He may view his responsibility not as standing above the moment but as realizing it fully. Hence his first task is to open himself to the actuality of that moment and to the norms and values that are given with that actuality. His question is then not what the past was in and for itself but what it is now for him in his existence. The result for the historical consciousness is comparable to the second mode of the scientific consciousness. Just as that mode undercut for the scientist the sense of the actuality of the nature from which he began, so this procedure undercuts for the historian the sense of the actuality of the past. The present alone is real—or perchance the envisioned future.

The scientific and the historical consciousness try to absorb and subordinate each other. The attempt on the part of the scientific consciousness to absorb the historical is the positivistic programme within history. The positivist recognizes that there is something cognitive and important about what the historian is doing, but he is convinced that in so far as it is cognitive and important it can be understood as a further extension of the scientific method. The simple assemblage of facts is an important prerequisite for the establishment of knowledge. But when the historian attempts to explain them, he must conform to the one logic of explanation that is everywhere applicable and has been best practised in the natural sciences. Here there is no difference between explanation and prediction. Hence for the historian to explain an event is for him to show that the event was in principle predictable. He can do this only by explicitly or implicitly appealing to general laws. These requisite laws are those now being worked out in social sciences. The historian can provide data for these sciences, and these sciences can provide explanatory laws for the historian. In this way human events can be brought within the body of unified science that is human knowledge. They can be freed from their bothersome involvement in unidirectional time.

The attempt of the historical consciousness to absorb the scientific can be called historicism. Viewed historically, science and the consciousness connected with it are seen to emerge out of definite historical conditions, and to have acted in their turn upon these conditions. The historical consciousness itself has a history. The science it has produced is viewed not as an independent entity but as a process of thought and the shaping of belief as these have proceeded through a community of human beings. The historian notes the changing shape of "nature" as human perception is altered by the growth of the sciences. To him positivism, and the positivist programme of absorbing history, are but one more historical phenomenon to be understood historically—that is, in terms of how they arose out of antecedent events and how they shape consequent events. Thus the whole of science is taken up into a temporally structured pattern of understanding.

In the preceding paragraphs I have used positivism to refer to the programme generated by the scientific consciousness to make itself the all-encompassing horizon of knowledge and to identify reality with what it knows. I have used historicism to refer to the parallel programme of the historical consciousness. The two programmes are in violent opposition to each other. Yet they have much in common. Both presuppose and articulate the consequences of the evaporation of transcendence or the death of God. That means that both vacillate between dogmatism and nihilism, between the absolutization of their apprehension of reality and their annihilation of their own truth and reality by the application of their methods also to themselves. On the whole nihilism is victorious. It is supported by the results that follow when either applies its methods to the other. In addition, absolutization of either vision leads to the brink of nihilism, for a science devoid of all human meaning is scarcely to be distinguished from nihilism, and the historicist who opens himself to the actuality of our present situation can hardly avoid being overwhelmed by its nihilistic spirit.

Young people are now in revolt against positivism and historicism. Many of them reject both the scientific and the historical forms of consciousness. They seek something else. The existentialist thought of Heidegger and Sartre served as a transition from the historical consciousness, but today that too has lost its power. Primitive, archaic, mystical and Eastern forms are more attractive.

The historical consciousness is able to survive only by transforming itself into utopianism. The past is felt as a burden, the present, as intolerable. But he who promises a quite different future gains a following. Since this future must be radically discontinuous with the past, and since God is culturally dead, the utopian consciousness is a revolutionary one for which even the best that history has produced must be swept away so that out of the resultant anarchy the sacred New will be born.

Unfortunately, both mysticism and utopianism only intensify the nihilistic consequences of positivism and historicism. They direct attention away from the most urgent problems of our time to unnatural psychic states and unrealizable goals. With all our preoccupation with science and history, and now with consciousness-expansion and a wholly new society, the food we eat, the water we drink, and the air we breathe have been beneath our notice. We have simply ignored the fact that the planetary supplies of these commodities are limited and that their replenishment requires conditions that we are rapidly destroying. We have known that we were poisoning our air, water and soil and using insecticides that destroy the natural enemies of pests while evolving new and immune species of the pests. But we have blithely ignored the realistic prophets of ecological doom, assuming that whenever we choose (why are we so slow to choose?) omniscient science and omnipotent technology can solve our problems.

Now as we enter a decade that may well see widespread famines and unparalleled misery, as well as accelerating and irreversible deterioration of the natural environment, we find ourselves unprepared. How can this have happened in a world in which scientific and historical knowledge is worshipped as God and in which everyone is talking incessantly of the future? What kind of insanity has caused us to use up vast amounts of irreplaceable resources to put men on the moon, when already the planet's population is outstripping its capacities to produce food?

I suggest that this insanity is rooted in our fundamental philosophies. For both the scientific and the historical consciousness, nature has lost all independent and real existence. Nature is an object of knowledge which exists only as it is grasped by science; or it is a function of changing human experience. Such a nature requires no respect. It is there to be endlessly exploited as the mere condition of human technology. It is presumably cyclical, inexhaustible and vacuous. If at some level of our consciousness we have "known" that we were rapidly destroying whole species of our fellow creatures, we have quickly consoled ourselves that this was the unfortunate consequence of "progress" and that science and technology would replace for us whatever was thereby lost. Since the reality or meaning of these animals was only what they were for us, it seemed that the problem was more to overcome our sentiments than to preserve our creaturely companions.

Protestant theologies have enthusiastically embraced the philosophical dichotomy of history and nature, even claiming that it expressed the biblical and Christian faith! Theologians have outdone philosophers in relegating nature to the realm of the indifferent. Twentieth-century Catholic theology, in its famous "transcendental turn", appears bent upon repeating and even exaggerating these Protestant errors.

In the years immediately ahead, positivism and historicism will collapse of their own dead weight as we are forced to reckon with the reality of the nature we have so long ignored. If we are to survive at all, we must develop a vision of our relation to nature quite opposite to that of both the scientific and the historical consciousness. We must operate in terms of an historical naturalism. As theologians, we must overcome the restriction of God to the horizon of history. The only God we can worship will be the God of *this* world in which nature and history are indissolubly united.

There have been movements in modernity that seemed to counter the general neglect and disparagement of nature. Marxism, for example, has emphasized the material basis for history. Yet in practice this has meant only a stress on economics as the substructure of culture and not any real interest in nature. Indeed, Marxism has been a major agent in overcoming the vestiges of respect for nature in archaic cultures. In recent decades there has been much talk of man's bodiliness and much deploring of the repression of the body. But the body in question has been chiefly the sensory and especially the sexual body. The body has not been seen in its kinship and vital interrelationship with its natural environment. Little has been said of the need of food, water and air.

A hundred years of evolutionary science have taught us that all life is intimately related and that nature as well as man is historical. Yet it is astonishing how superficially these truths have penetrated our consciousness. The evolutionary philosophers who sought to reshape our self-understanding are not regarded as sufficiently rigorous to be taken quite seriously by the scientific mentality, for which a non-historical mathematical physics is still the paradigm of true knowledge. And the historical consciousness has continued to divorce nature from the sphere of its interest except as human opinions and discoveries about nature enter into history.

Furthermore, even the evolutionary thinkers have failed us at the crucial point. Teilhard de Chardin is here an all-too-typical case. No one has more powerfully depicted the dynamic movement of natural history from which man has arisen and of which, therefore, man is a part. Yet with the rise of man Teilhard sees all reality and meaning and movement focused in him alone. The rest of nature becomes the mere condition of his further development. There is no need to attend further to these conditions. They take care of themselves, or else man through his intelligence modifies them to suit his good pleasure. Indeed, Teilhard teaches that in the end the noosphere will achieve so great an independence from its physical and biological conditions that their ultimate destruction is of no importance. Meanwhile, these conditions constitute no limit upon man's multiplication and filling of the earth. For Teilhard the question how such men shall eat and drink and breathe does not occur.

But these questions will arise with apocalyptic force in the decade now beginning, and all our history will have to be rewritten in their light. We will need a planetary history in which man appears as a part of nature, dependent upon it, worshipping it, mastering it, exploiting it and ignoring it, until he discovers that he has fearfully disrupted the natural conditions that sustain his life. Christianity and the Church will have to be viewed in

terms of their vast contribution to this total development. Protestantism must bear the greatest guilt for furthering the scientific
and historical modes of consciousness and for liberating them
from the restraints of religion. Catholicism must bear the fearful
burden that long after the crisis was plain it continued to oppose
in the name of nature and humanity those restraints upon man
which alone could have mitigated the disasters that could no
longer be avoided.

Many will be tempted to abjure the Christian faith rather than
to bear such burdens of guilt. But where can they turn? Marxism,
nationalism, capitalism and secular humanism are fully involved
in the guilt, and they are far poorer in resources for repentance
and conversion than is Christianity. Shall we turn then to primi-
tivism or mysticism? But they offer at best a private, temporary
evasion of historical catastrophe. Once human life has been radically historicized neither a pre-historic nor a post-historic consciousness affords real escape. The attempt to escape will only
accelerate the rush to final doom. Science and technology must
be made to subserve human ends. They must not be abandoned.
Having used them to wound nature we must employ them in the
effort to nurse her back to health.

We will be forced to make delicate and appalling political
decisions which will require the wisdom of the fully informed
historical consciousness along with repudiation of its limitations.
Those who turn their back upon history will be useless and worse
than useless. Similarly, utopian goals, whether political or religious, must be abandoned in favour of concerted realistic efforts
to save humanity from self-destruction.

If Christianity does not survive and recover health through
repentance, it is hard to see how the love of life, apart from which
man cannot survive, will be nurtured. What is needed is a love
of all life beginning with the biological level and encompassing
all men and all dimensions of human aliveness. Such a love must
be asserted again and again against extreme temptations to seize
short-run and narrowly selfish advantages at the expense of the
future and of fellow man. It must be asserted as the basis on
which through the terrors of the time of famines there can be
kindled a will to live that has almost vanished during our time

of prosperity. Such a will to live must be experienced as in harmony with the ultimate nature of things, that is, with God himself. We will be in urgent need of a hope that is neither utopian nor apocalyptic, and such a hope cannot be distinguished from faith in God.

C. W. Mönnich

Church History in the Context of the Human Sciences

How does Church history fit into the whole complex of human sciences? Every Church historian uses them. Human phenomena are scattered all over the field which he covers professionally, and these phenomena are explained to him by sociology and psychology, by economics and the science of politics, by linguistics and stylistics. Church history cannot reduce these human phenomena to timeless abstractions without depriving them of their substantial truth. Whatever definition of the Church we start from, we always have to deal with human realities, not with data that float around somewhere in space beyond time. Whether we see the Church as an unchangeable sacramental value, or as God's people on its way to the peace of the Kingdom, as static or dynamic, the Church cannot be contained in a kind of mathematical pattern composed of eternally valid situations. Even the most rigid view of the Church as firmly founded on the rock of ages must embody the concept of the *eschaton*, "until the end".

Because of this, every image, every pronouncement, every event and every person, is related to something beyond itself, and is a moment that points away from itself towards the Lord who is more than his Church in that he embodies the future.

The Church as the subject of Church history is always the Church of people who live in a political, social, economic, cultural and psychological framework. This fact makes it impossible for Church history to do without these human sciences, since they provide the very tools for its research. More important, they provide the relevant questions with which the historian has to deal.

And, most important of all perhaps, they provide the norms by which to criticize any form of historiography, also that of the Church, since all historical writing runs the risk of turning historical reality into an ideology or mythology.

Let us look at an illustration of this. According to the rule of St Benedict of Nursia the abbot must be a father to his monks, caring for the weak and avoiding tyranny, and he must be obeyed by the monks as if he were Christ himself.

This image no doubt already implies a particular theological attitude, but one that already embodies a centuries-old conviction about the imitation of Christ. This theology in turn reflects the belief that saw in the martyr the victorious follower of Christ in his triumph, and in the monk the successor to the martyr.

But this raises several questions. What are the circumstances that lead to persecution? What causes a group of people to see the death of its victims as that type of triumph? Where do we draw the line between ordinary hero-worship and the veneration due to a martyr (more than mere hero-worship)? How did the ascetic become the successor to the martyr? In other words: why and how did the command to imitate Christ come to develop on these particular lines? Sociology and psychology will not be able to supply the whole answer, but no answer can do without their findings.

Let us hold on for a moment to this example taken from the rule of St Benedict. The image of the abbot as given in the rule is clearly different from that of the Desert Fathers or of Irish monasticism. It can hardly be doubted that behind the picture given us in the rule of St Benedict there lies considerable pastoral experience. Is it then not obvious that the historian should consult the man who knows something about pastoral psychology?

And then we have the question of how this image of the abbot worked out in history. How did it lead to such fascinating interpretations as given by the great medieval abbots such as Rhabanus Maurus, Suger of St Denis or Peter the Venerable? And if they do not correspond to the original image, can we dispose of the matter simply by pointing to human weakness? Even if this were the case, should it not be investigated? Where and how did it arise?

These people wielded spiritual and political power, and we

have to understand them in the framework of Carolingian society or of the feudal system: an agrarian world about which we get our information from historical sociography, the history of law and of politics. Only when we have some idea about how a ruler would have to behave in such a world, what kind of rules he was subjected to in such a society, what kind of demands were made on him, can we say anything meaningful about him as abbot in Church history.

Those who practise the human sciences are increasingly interested in linguistics and statistics, and this means that these two subjects are also becoming more important for Church history. Even in early Christianity, linguistic studies played their part, not only because most Christian authors went through a thorough training in rhetoric, but particularly because the problem of hermeneutics was inextricably tied up with the proclamation. We may here think of the various translations of the Bible, or of the difficulties that beset the missionaries working among the Slavs in the ninth century, who had to deal with the theological meaning of the texts concerning the Babylonian confusion of tongues, the trilingual inscription on the cross and the gift of tongues at Pentecost.

So far we have only shown that modern Church history has to make use of the technical assistance provided by the human sciences. But there is more to it than a question of technique. The application of methods and insights acquired by the human sciences to Church history also means that we believe we *can* somehow apply those methods and insights, in other words, that, in principle, we cannot draw a hard and fast line separating the subject-matter of these sciences from that of Church history.

The reality studied by those sciences and by Church history is the same: the reality of man's behaviour. It is on this point that the common interest converges. The institutions that influence the life of Church members are the very instruments that shape their behaviour and make or mar their search for the *eschaton* of God's peace. And this *eschaton* itself is not an institution but a person: the Messiah himself.

This applies also when these institutions—the ecclesiastical hierarchical structure, dogma and liturgy—are seen as factors that rest in one way or another on God's revelation. For this revelation is none other than the human incarnation of the Messiah, the just, and the body in which he continues to live, a body composed of people above all, and not primarily of institutions and documents that are detached from man's existence and relegated to a sphere of supernatural validity. The law is made for man, not the other way about. Man is not a puppet dancing at the end of legal and institutional strings.

It is of fundamental importance to see that Church history cannot be detached from universal history and locked up in a separate existence. It is not only technically difficult to determine what exactly is "Church" and what is not. I shall not deal here with the problems of method on this point, such problems as: how should we deal with groups that have seceded—as splinter-groups off a monolithic block, or as groups that belong to the great indivisible Church in a way we cannot discern? Should we talk about Church history, or would it be better to talk about the history of Christianity?

It is therefore not only technically difficult to mark off in precise terms the field covered by Church history, but if we had such a starting-point, it would still suffer from a dangerous weakness of method. Even if we took the widest possible view of Church history as the history of all those phenomena to which we could apply the name "Christian", we would still not do justice to the scriptural fact that the just Servant of Yahweh does not lead an isolated existence.

The body of Christ is clearly not isolated. According to the Bible, the relation between God and mankind is not bilateral but triangular: God—Moses or the prophets—the people; God—God's people—the nations; God—the Messiah—the world. This triangular structure is embodied even in the great commandment: "You must love the Lord your God with all your heart, with all your soul and with all your mind. This is the greatest and the first commandment. The second resembles it: you must love your neighbour as yourself. On these two commandments hang the whole Law, and the Prophets also" (Matt. 22. 37–40).

It is the just man that God loves, not the religious virtuoso. But this just man is only just because of his attitude to his neighbour.

He does not have this love in himself, he is not the *beatus possidens*, the happy possessor, who, out of the fullness of his association with God, now philanthropically distributes his treasures to his neighbour; he receives his justice through his association with his neighbour, who is also Christ's neighbour, even Christ himself.

Christ himself is not without his body, and this body cannot exist in isolation. In Church history this means that the Church as the body of Christ can only be written about in connection with the history of mankind. In less theological terms: Church history only makes sense when seen as integrated in the whole history of mankind. It is the history of mankind's search for God's kingdom and its justice.

This is not a value judgment but an angle from which we look at things. Whoever confesses the name of Christ puts himself under the judgment of the Just One and is involved in imitating him. Church history then becomes the story of the drama of God's justice in the history of the world.

This angle is not a new one: it is the apocalyptic angle so sharply brought out by St Augustine. Here, too, this greatest of Western Fathers of the Church is still pertinent. It is also the story of Christian failure, of wandering and erring, of the provisional character of events, of the longing for the fleshpots of Egypt, of the rude awakenings from the sweet dreams of fulfilment.

One may well ask whether, seen from this angle, Church history does not get hopelessly blurred. If we take it that the interpersonal relationships of mankind, seen in the light of messianic justice, constitute the subject-matter of Church history, its scope seems to become exceedingly vague. How then does it differ from history in general?

The Church historian will frequently run into this difficulty. In early Christianity an ecumenical council was a council convoked by the emperor and concerned with affairs that affected the whole of his empire. The historian will then first ask himself how it is that a Christian empire considered itself as the "inhabited world", and only then how far the message of such a council was addressed to the whole of mankind.

Another example: where does one draw the line between

Church history and world history in the Investiture struggle? Or, in a more modest situation: how far does the behaviour of a bishop endowed with secular power still belong to Church history? We need not go into specific questions here, but the underlying problem of where and how Church history differs from general history remains.

One might counter this with a question from the other end: why do we want Church history to have its own separate subject-matter? Put in such general terms, the question is relevant to the whole of history. It is in fact a question about the image of the past. What do we look for in history? A really clear picture of the past which we can draw by detaching ourselves from it? A clear description of a stage with recognizable and therefore relatively constant characters?

In Holland this question about the image and nature of history has frequently been asked, particularly by J. Huizinga, and, in an instructive interview, by J. Romein and his followers. The result has been greater clarity.

They see history as a gathering of manifold data in a comprehensive view, where the historian does not merely register mechanically what has happened but re-creates the reality of history, of which he thus creates an "image". The great historians were indeed creative minds whose labour was clearly influenced by the power of literary imagination.

Here, however, also lies the relativity of that picture or image. It can help the historian to forecast the future: it provides him with a kind of crystal ball; but it is this undeniable presence of the historian in his work which makes it also subjective and may lead to a fixation of what was a prophetic image of history into an ideology which must then perpetuate what has been achieved in the past. As Romein puts it, the image must constantly be crushed in order not to become an obstacle to further progress.

But this view that the image of history must constantly be crushed, again leads to the question whether historiography and historical research are limited to this setting up of an image. The real point is the historian's involvement in his material? The historian is part and parcel of the reality he studies. He is not only trying to discover the past in general, but also, and particularly, his own past, and even that is not all. He is looking for his own identity. For him history is one of the human sciences where he tries to discover the identity of man, and, by implication, his own.

A true historian cannot really work on the lines of Leopold von Ranke's concept according to which the historian tries to find out "how it really happened" in the past. He just does not have the means to come to a conclusive total view. Documents have been lost, unknown factors have played their part, and even if he had an ideal situation and all the sources at his disposal, he would still be at a disadvantage and even remain totally alienated from the past because he cannot bridge the gap: the people he deals with did not know the outcome, but he does.

It is not only impossible to arrive at a satisfactory reconstruction of the past because of the documentation—too meagre, as the student of antiquity or the Middle Ages knows only too well, or so abundant as to be unmanageable, as the student of our recent times finds out. There is above all the impossibility to create the necessary distance from the subject.

For a man who knows that he exists in and through his relatedness to others it is difficult to form an "image" of the Church. He can, however, involve himself in people of the past.

For him, too, the time factor differs from that of the great nineteenth-century historians. For the essential objectivity of the age was useful in that it allowed him to dissociate himself from his subject-matter and so to attempt an almost film-like historically reliable portrait of the past.

When, however, we start from the historian's involvement with the people of the past, the time-factor becomes something different. It is no longer the measure of the distance between the historian and the image he sees, but rather a specific dimension of anthropology.

The historian then is an anthropologist, somebody who practises one of the human sciences, only differing from the others in that they work with the data of living people, such as statistics, psychological observation, ethnological patterns—in brief, with contemporary matter, while he works with data from the past, data provided by archaeology, the languages of the past, the documents of a society that no longer exists: he works with non-contemporary material.

These words, contemporary and non-contemporary, only indicate a formal difference. The difference acquires substance and viability only when we know how the time-factor works in history.

Time is not the dimension which makes it possible to provide the consecutive unfolding of a series of moving pictures. I have already pointed out that this leads to a kind of history writing which is no longer very useful to us.

The involvement of the historian who sets out deliberately to create a picture of the past is in fact of the aesthetic kind. He observes from without and his involvement arises mainly from his wish to satisfy his sense of beauty. And just as we do not accept this detachment in our experience of beauty, so we reject it in our concept of history.

The involvement at work in history is of another kind. It is born in an encounter with the past, an encounter which makes us fully human. For man is not a creature complete in itself; he only becomes complete in his relationship with others.

This is in fact also the basis of the human sciences in general. To refrain from making "value judgments" helps the student in his search, but it is not his real preoccupation, if he wishes to be integrated as a man of science and not keep his scientific activity so drastically separated from the rest of his personality that he becomes schizophrenic. But what, then, is the meaning of this dimension of time, with which the historian happens to be permanently saddled?

To find this out we must constantly remember that the history we are here talking about is the history of people, of human persons. This means that the lines of the development of the non-human reality—the lines of geology and biology—do not really serve our purpose.

First of all, the evolutionary processes at work in geology and biology are far too slow to provide us with any scale that could apply to the course of historical events. When we observe in nature any acceleration of the evolutionary processes it is practically always due to human activity, as when man intervenes in the management of land, the exploitation of mineral resources, the extermination of animal species, and so on.

Secondly, man's activity shows uncertainty, an uncertainty

4—c.

which we can interpret theologically as a sign of his freedom: he can always do something else. That is why the historical processes cannot be repeated while in the natural sciences repetitiveness is an integral part of the method.

Time, then, is not just the dimension within which predictable processes take place, but also the dimension within which man's choice operates. Ultimately, he is responsible for his own future. I say "ultimately" because there are obviously certain physical laws to which man is subject because he is also part of nature. The length of a generation is a natural datum which has obviously to be reckoned with when, for instance, we investigate the duration of certain phenomena in human culture.

But the datum of uncertainty, the lack of definiteness in man's existence, is also important. The time-dimension of history implies the factor of contingency.

Man is clearly determined by his past and the past of his species. But he is also determined by the uncertainty of his future. If man's involvement with his fellow humans is essential for his existence, then he is involved in the life of the other, and this means that he is involved in the future. For we live for the future, just as we are determined by our past.

This implies for the historian that the problems with which he is concerned are determined by the question of what in the past had a future and what not. It is his specific task, as a practitioner of one of the human sciences, to examine this question. The line of time is the line of man's existence as such. It embraces not only time in its chronological sense, but also time as the sphere within which man has to build his future.

When we apply this to ecclesiastical historiography, we may say that the formal aspect of the concept of the future as an essential moment in history can be worked out substantially: it is a characteristic feature of Christianity that it conceives of the future as the coming of the Messiah and his kingdom.

This does not mean that the Church historian is entitled to sit in judgment on history. No science has the means to pass an ethical or religious judgment on the reality which it investigates. It can no doubt provide evidence for such a judgment, just as it can suggest means to do the right thing and avoid evil in practice. But it is the Church historian's duty to show how the concept of the future, seen as the realization of God's kingdom and its justice, has fared in practice in the past. Church history is the history of a judgment and of man's part in that judgment, namely, the judgment of the Messiah.

Justice is the ultimate ground of the Church historian's task, the justice that signifies salvation and peace. The concept of this justice in view of the future is certainly not a blueprint, sent down ready-made from some celestial drawing-office, and handed to mankind for execution.

Mankind is always on the move towards the future, and cannot do otherwise, for death besets its past and death appears in the present if it stops moving towards the future. Man has a vision, a dream, a poetic image of the kingdom of God, nor do Christians see the future any more clearly.

There are citizens of the kingdom whose names do not appear in the ecclesiastical registers. There are saints among the pagans —that is the way the early Church understood Job. Time and again we find that we simply do not know where the dividing line runs between Church history and world history, particularly so when we look at the situation with the eyes of the Church.

Every form Christianity assumes in history stands under the judgment of the Messiah. But this judgment implies the future also: the future as protest against injustice, as the will to go forward, as the motive to live on for those who, in spite of the past of the various Christian communities and their ways of life, in other words, in spite of being burdened with death, refused to reject the Messiah. Such people did not know the future and may not even have tried to calculate it in the form of plans for the future.

None of us knows the future, not even the futurologist who, at best, is a super-planner, but often also the victim of science-fiction. But living mankind lives on the future of which it dreams. In so far as Christianity is alive, it lives on the future of the justice of the Messiah. That is why eternal life is the *terminus ad quem* of Church history, but not its subject-matter. The Church historian has nothing to do with the visions of the young men and the dreams of the old ones, of which Joel 2. 28 speaks—but Joel 2. 28 is very much concerned with Church history.

What, then, must the Church historian do? Exactly the same

as every other man of science does: investigate his subject-matter on the points that are relevant, and relevant are those points that have something to do with the struggle for justice.

He will not fight his human fight as an academic historian, but, informed by Church history about man and his struggle for the future, he can certainly be a fighter.

Insight into the social structures or psychological mechanisms does not by itself procure a better society or mental health. But these analyses are necessary if he wants to stand as man among men: he must be involved in their lives and their future.

Secondly, since most research in the human sciences is concerned with our present age, with the contemporary aspect of human reality, he has to point out that there is also a non-contemporary dimension to man; that man moves along the lines of time, that is: from the not-yet to fulfilment.

It is particularly on this latter point that the Church historian will find that he has to take up a critical attitude towards his colleagues in the human sciences. The preoccupation with the contemporary situation, particularly in sociology, economics and the science of politics, can cling too exclusively to the methodically most valuable principle of "research without value judgments", but by the same token lead to a fixation of the picture or image and so wrongly suggest that "whatever is, is right". When that happens these sciences can only too easily become means in the hands of those who want to manipulate mankind for their own purposes.

By drawing attention to the non-contemporary aspect of man, the factor of the future as an essential dimension of man's existence, a factor which is primary in historical investigation, the one-sidedness and dangers of an exclusive concentration on the contemporary situation can be avoided. Church history can add to this that there is a human conviction, a human belief, which sees the future as the achievement and fulfilment of justice.

Translated by Theo Westow

Bernard Plongeron

Church History as the Point of Intersection of Religious Studies

WHO could fail to be struck by the paradox that whereas, on the one hand, it is becoming more and more common for the concepts of the "meaning, philosophy and theology" of history to appear in journals of religious studies, on the other a great many people are less interested than ever in being taught Church history?

One ought, of course, to take into account the fact that people today are frequently fascinated by man in relation to the future he is making by disengaging himself from the past. To justify this naïve outlook they point, not without reason, to a concept of history so burdened by tradition, with all that it implies of rigid fixity, that it is as it were "dead". On the other hand, their enthusiasm returns when Church history can be seen to hold the keys to the problems of our time.

One deduction from this is that the pace of cultural change as we know it today radically alters the criteria of knowledge: religious studies, like other sciences, recognize that their specific identity no longer depends on a few factors borrowed from history. The problem, because it involves the nature of knowledge more than the content of knowledge, demands a pooling of resources to replace the false autonomies characteristic of the departmentalized teaching of the theological "treatises". In fact religious studies are instinctively returning to an examination of the Church's millennial history with a view to working out, each from its own particular angle (dogma, ethics, spirituality, liturgy,

canon law, and so on), a Christian anthropology capable of nour-
ishing their methodological considerations.

In order to do this, religious studies are naturally turning to
historians—to give direction to their work, not as a substitute.
The image of the crossroads or point of intersection is supposed
to suggest precisely that. It implies various paths converging, and
new directions.

Clearly, the central point must be fixed, which is another way
of saying that religious history must have stability. In spite of
noticeable attempts to improve matters,[1] Church history, seen in
terms of its specific identity as a turn-table for the other religious
disciplines, still calls for a radically new approach on the part of
those who study it. This article thus points mainly to the need to
recognize a dual crisis: that presented by historical language becoming open to contributions from the other human sciences,
and the crisis involved in the search of religious studies for their
historical foundations. Precisely from within this dual crisis religious studies and history will come to a greater understanding
of the nature and extent of the dialogue between them.

I. Brief Reflections on a Joint Crisis

The historian who disregards the construction of these foundations is thus challenged by the very disciplines which for so long
merely demanded of him that he translate their own methodology
in terms of dates, facts and erudite descriptions of controversies.
An historical study of our manuals and courses of Church history
will one day disclose just how much historical discourse has been
enclosed within the syllogistic frameworks of an all-embracing
theology. As soon as the latter dissolved under the pressure of our
pluralist society, it naturally also spelt the ruin of a concept of

---

[1] See, for an outline of concrete cases of religious history undergoing
osmosis with the theological disciplines, L. Febvre, *Au cœur religieux du
XVIe siècle* (Paris, 1957) and especially, *Le problème de l'incroyance au
XVIe siècle* (Paris, 1968 edition). On the specific role of Church history,
M. de Certeau, "L'histoire religieuse du XVIIe siècle. Problèmes de
méthodes", in *Rech. Sc. relig.*, 57 (1969), pp. 231–50. Compare with R.
Guelluy, "L'evolution des méthodes théologiques à Louvain d'Erasme à
Jansenius", in *Rev. Hist. Eccl.*, 37 (1941), pp. 31–144.

Church history which, veering uneasily between the history of theology and historical theology, had to some extent lost its identity. At this stage the crisis became a joint one and necessitated a new approach.

1. *A Concept undergoing Change*

An historian as celebrated as P. Goubert has challenged an attitude which, although he has in mind particularly the Church of France at the end of the *ancien régime*, we cannot be sure no longer exists in our own day. "Only rarely, in this country which has remained Catholic, has anyone had the courage to stress the fact that the Roman Catholic Church in France remained the unshakeable champion of a global notion of the world—embracing nature, man, science, education—in which everything had been calmly settled in advance at least since St Thomas."[2]

As if echoing this opinion of a lay expert, the Archbishop of Gorizia in Italy, Mgr A. Pangrazio, went even further in his indictment of a "description of the Catholic Church" before the bishops attending Vatican II. "The Catholic Church is described in too static and abstract a way, and too little place is given to the dynamic and concrete, historical aspect of the Church.... The mystery of the history of the Church is insufficiently conveyed, in my opinion." This churchman did not baulk at taking the historian imprisoned in an all-embracing theology to task: "In the history of the Church, through the action of the Holy Spirit and with the co-operation, or else on occasion because of the resistance, of men, events follow one another in an unlikely and unexpected fashion which no theological system can either foresee or later integrate. Who among the great theologians of the thirteenth century, for example, would have thought the great Western schism which was to split the Church in the sixteenth century possible, and who among them could have foreseen the corruption and abuses which disfigured the Church in the period preceding the Reformation? And, conversely, who could have foreseen at the time of the Reformation the

[2] P. Goubert, *L'Ancien Régime: Vol. 1: La Société (1600–1750)* (Paris, 1969), p. 254.

astonishing consolidation of the Church brought about by God's grace after the Council of Trent?"[3]

In what follows we will deal with three basic accusations raised in this passage, concerning the notions of duration, space and the "concrete" element (in other words language) in the historical development of the Church.

2. *Historical Duration and an Institutional Church*

Canon lawyers, philosophers and theologians are all interested in the apparent antinomy between dynamism and "the structural", in other words religious institutions. Too often described in formal and juridical terms, these institutions seem, by their sheer impenetrableness, to cast a veil over the dynamism which historians are discovering at every stage in the free-play of human freedoms being exercised: motivation and deciding factors. Religious institutions would represent more the result or consequence of certain lines of development. They are wrongly taken to symbolize what is ready-made, because they share in the "mystery" of the history of the Church. It is of no avail for us to know everything there is to know about the conditions surrounding the founding and the geographical setting of the religious orders from the tenth to the thirteenth centuries, when we can miss the essential if writers of manuals and teachers pass over in silence the dynamic developments leading from splendour to decadence. Historical examples tell us a great deal: first the order of Cluny was created, then it fell into decadence at least to the extent that it warranted a wholehearted attack by St Bernard directed against the corruption of the monks of that order; thereupon the Cistercian order took over with its strict rule and organization. But it too came to contain abuses and was undermined by them, by its collective wealth; it was then the turn of the mendicant orders who later came up against the same dangers. Must one then rest content with noting this dialectic between life and death leading to the conclusion that an institution—even a religious one—seems destined to fall into decadence as soon as it is left to itself? In that case, a glance afforded by the historian at the principal dates and structures of the institution (or doctrinal system) will provide

[3] Translated from the French text in *Discours au Concile Vatican II* (Paris, 1964), pp. 199–202.

information for (rather than "mould") the other disciplines on the meaning of historical duration. A period of historical duration begins when the historian detects circumstances in which the collective faith of Christians can give life to a fact which is historically dead and strictly local to the point of actually giving it new dimensions.

The approach remains typically historical when at the heart of the event in question there appears a personality of transcendent influence. The relation between the man and the institution could provide a fruitful means of rehabilitating both biography and the recording of events which are nowadays unjustly decried. If we distinguished a particular event fixed and identified in time (*le ponctuel*) and its long-term effects (*le continu*) we should see that the important thing was perhaps not Francis of Assisi and the founding of his order in 1209 but rather the Franciscan revolution which renewed the evangelical values and the spiritual and cultural expressions of the Christian conscience in the thirteenth century; we would sense why that was possible in the thirteenth century and not in the twelfth; we would understand the change undergone by these values in the ups and downs which form the threads of individual and collective destinies. Vincent de Paul in the seventeenth century, Fr. Peyriguère at the turn of the twentieth, not to mention Fr Chevrier, personify the revelation for their time, and suited to the needs of their contemporaries in the faith, of the face of Christ, the Son of God, of the God of history. The reverberations set up by these personalities in the world of their time would become, at least in their most concrete and hence (thanks to the different historical approaches) most easily identifiable aspects, a sort of epiphany for "those with eyes to see".[4]

[4] F. de Beer, *La conversion de saint François selon Thomas de Celano* (Paris, 1963). From a comparative analysis of vocabulary the author notes that in the first life of St Francis by Thomas of Celano poverty is an experience encountered by the Franciscan community after the first journey to the Pope, hence the curious lack of determination about it in the rule of 1209. It was in the first days of learning to live by begging in Rome that Franciscan poverty became at the same time (the second life of St Francis) normative and mystical in aspiration.

The challenge to the Christian conscience presented by a phenomenon fixed and identified in time is equally palpable in J. F. Six, *Charles de Foucauld aujourd'hui* (Paris, 1966). But the same author's doctoral thesis,

3. A Socio-cultural Approach to Religious Ideologies

But "to see" in historical terms means to locate or more precisely to circumscribe the area proper to the specific nature and development of one type of problem in religious history. Professional theologians would willingly abandon certain intellectual generalizations if, say, historians put forward a socio-cultural pinpointing of religious ideologies. Such an approach can be seen in various guises. In studying the seventeenth century, M. de Certeau stresses the "more or less secret networks in which the same ideas circulated—either Jansenist or emanating from the *spirituels* or the *dévots*; the free-thinking or erudite 'circles' made up of a relatively homogeneous group of people whose activities were occult; the social and professional specialization of the religious congregations which gradually took on recognizable positions in the social hierarchy and functions which served to differentiate them more clearly. Partitioning therefore took place between members of small private circles (themselves cut-off from public 'reason') or between groups henceforth more clearly determined by objective tasks, in connection with the milieux from which their members were recruited and by means of the ideologies which became the sign of this particularization."[5]

Such an attempt properly to situate a problem historically would equip religious studies with a socio-cultural tool while at the same time remedying a methodological gap recognized by all. Three approaches could contribute to this: analysis by theme of the ecclesiastical press and of the religious content of certain political periodicals; an examination, within the context of the confessional plurality of a region, of "religious boundaries"; and above all a study in depth of language in which language is seen structurally in connection with the vocabulary used by apologists and polemicists or as an aid or obstacle to acceptance of the Christian message in a nonconformist environment, for example in a missionary country.

Un prêtre, Antoine Chevrier, fondateur du Prado (1826–1879) (Paris, 1965), shows the risks of extrapolations. The interpretation consists in defending a modern concept of evangelization against the spirituality of the nineteenth century, hence the anachronisms in the vocabulary and in certain thematic analyses.

[5] M. de Certeau, *art. cit.*, pp. 241–2.

Obviously dogmatic and moral theologians would be in a better position to grasp the nature of a problem which has been situated historically if historians did not merely go over the description given of it by the great theorists of the time. How did the theological thought of the clerical and lay *élites* come to be diffused to the masses? How much of it was understood by Christian people in formulas simplified and rendered less flexible in order to make a collective impact? In the course of the transformations it undergoes, is the true question at stake (the disputes about grace, the notion of the Church, the Christian's moral duties, and so on...) posed in the same way that scholars had first debated it? The case of Pascal, the writer of the *Provinciales*, should make us think. I have, personally, conducted several seminars of theologians anxious to explore the collective attitudes peculiar to the Jansenist journal *Les Nouvelles Ecclésiastiques*: the historical approaches to the doctrinal content did not fail to surprise those taking part who had been imbued at the start with ideological outlines which took on a different shade after a study of the documents themselves.[6] Raymond Deniel, for his part, has sought to bring out the image of the family reflected in the Catholic press in the France of the Restoration. He has used four publications: *Le Conservateur* (founded by Chateaubriand in October 1818), *La Quotidienne* (July 1815), *Le Mémorial catholique* (January 1824) and above all the unofficial journal of the French clergy of the Restoration, *L'Ami de la Religion et du Roi*. All the analyses prove how far theologians, pastors and moralists rely upon a religious ideal based on a political outlook, in this case that of the traditionalists, Chateaubriand, Bonald, Lamennais, Genoude.[7]

It would be tempting to favour an approach based on national boundaries, whereas in fact historians should reconstitute the geography of mental entities. We should deal not now with the State but with "the province". Sometimes a cultural and religious "province" includes several states (in this sense one can speak of the revolution of the Atlantic world in the eighteenth century), sometimes it denotes firm religious boundaries within one State.

[6] B. Plongeron, "Une image de l'Eglise d'après les 'Nouvelles Ecclésiastiques' 1728–1790", in *Rev. Hist. Egl. de France*, 151 (1967), pp. 241–68.

[7] R. Deniel, *Une image de la famille et de la société sous la Restauration* (Paris, 1965).

This is highly important as regards religious feeling in particular: that associated with the humanism of the South should not, according to rivals of Henri Bremond, be located south of some border between Italy and France—something we should remember when it comes to revolutionary claims upon the Papal State of Comtat-Venaissin—but between a Southern and a Northern France. The humanism of the North, worked on by the *devotio moderna* which had such a profound influence in Spain at the end of the Middle Ages, related, in several countries of Northeastern Europe, to a biblical and patristic tradition of the Christian life.[8] The unity of a doctrinal and spiritual system is broken by other boundaries, as has been shown in the case of the Jansenism in Lorraine.[9] Such an attempt geographically to situate spiritual entities sharing a homogeneous socio-cultural context would open up a new path for the theology of spirituality which would then be doctrinally and sociologically enlightened and no longer merely the product of the influence of one author upon another.

Thus a dialectic would be established between what is "given" by the *élites* and what is "received"—and "lived"—by the Christian masses. Specialists in Christian anthropology would have their bit to say concerning the psychology of different peoples and group dynamics, especially when tackling the following:

4. Languages and the Formation of Doctrinal Concepts in the Course of History

It is doubtful whether any branch of study today has failed to pose to itself the problem of language. Church historians cannot escape it by sticking to a way of forming doctrinal concepts inherited from theology.

The attention which has been paid to the relationship of the Roman Church to the civilizations it has encountered is of special

---

[8] M. Venard, "Histoire littéraire et sociologie historique: deux voies pour l'histoire religieuse", in *Actes du Colloques d'Aix* (March, 1966), pp. 78-9. A. Weiler, "Scholasticism and Christian Renaissance Humanism", in *Concilium* (September 1967), pp. 41-3 (American edn., vol. 27).

[9] R. Taveneaux, *Le Jansénisme en Lorraine 1640-1789* (Paris, 1960). From this exemplary work P. Chaunu has drawn the necessary conclusions for our purpose in an article entitled "Jansénisme et frontière de catholicité (XVIIe et XVIIIe siècles). A propos du jansénisme lorrain", in *Rev. Hist.*, 227 (1962), pp. 115-38.

interest to the history of catechetics, as is shown by Bartomeu
Melia's fine study of the evangelization of Paraguay in the seventeenth and eighteenth centuries. Because the language of the
settlers was Castilian, the Jesuit missionaries sought to make contact with the colonized people, the Indians, in their own language, namely Guarini. "For the missionary, grammar is a sacred
science; no evangelization without translation. Making a cate-
chism and making a grammar are simply two aspects of one and
the same missionary effort."[10] The social criterion thereby overlaps with the religious since, by refusing to use the language of
the occupying people (if we consider the settler for the time being
as a Spaniard), the missionary deliberately associated opposition
to the Spanish language with opposition to colonial rule.

Whereas missionary theology readily accepted this slide from
the religious into the social, dogmatic theologians showed themselves to be more cautious when it came to the criterion of heresy,
in other words of the deposit of faith. Yet modern Church historians note that, under the influence of different forms of pluralism, the Mystical Body has broken up into several Churches: a
decisive factor has been that a notorious heretic can become an
official Church minister, in another Church. The one certainty
spreads out into certainties in the plural through the multiplication of professions of faith in which mental representations of
the Church to which one belongs have as much importance as
the doctrinal substance of the credo adhered to. A non-religious
type of certainty emerges, under these circumstances, from participation in civil society. Protestants and Catholics, Jesuits and
Jansenists all undergo this evolution in the course of the increasingly politicized eighteenth century.[11] In extreme cases the socio-
cultural expression of the group is of more weight than the subject of a dogmatic controversy, hence the need to study the different vocabularies under the two headings of the explicit (what
is said) and the implicit (what causes that to be said).

With history as intermediary, new links can thus be created

[10] B. Melia, *La création d'un langage chrétien dans les réductions des
Guarini au Paraguay*, thesis written for the Catholic theological faculty in
Strasbourg (1969), p. 93.
[11] Cf. B. Plongeron, *Conscience religieuse en Révolution* (Paris, 1969):
"heresy" or the socio-cultural status of ecclesiology, pp. 192–211.

between anthropology and dogma on condition that we reflect on another dimension which has still to emerge fully into the light of day, and which we shall deal with in the following section.

II. Historical Events and the "Mystery" of the Church

1. *History and Dogma*

God is no different in the twentieth century from what he was in the paleolithic age. There is, however, a history of men's ideas of God, of the rituals through which they have sought to enter into communion with him, of the ascetic practices by means of which they have tried to experience his presence. Certain developments are discernible in this history. One can even say that progress is made in getting to know the object in question, namely God, suggested by the passage from primitive religions to the great monotheisms.

In an analogous way it is possible to speak of a history of dogma. Once again we start from something given: the fact of Christ as presented in the witness of the apostles. This fact as such is immutable. On the other hand, history registers a progress in men's understanding of this datum which is part of the "mystery of the Church", the fullness of Christ. Cardinal Daniélou admits that the history of dogma had some difficulty in getting itself recognized. He notes the indignation aroused by Jules Lebreton's book, *Histoire du dogme de la Trinité*. While Loisy published *L'Evangile et l'Eglise*, Blondel replied with *Histoire et Dogme*. The victim of an exaggerated historicism, Loisy thought religious truth was dependent upon the age in which it was formulated, that it therefore had no permanent value. Well, "it is not truth which changes, as Loisy thought, nor the spirit which evolves, but language which becomes more precise".[12] Perhaps one should add that there is more than just language becoming more precise: there are different approaches being made towards the same object. This, however, did not prevent historians and theologians after the modernist crisis from shutting themselves up in a rigid attitude of prudence nourished by a reciprocal

---

[12] J. Daniélou, "Histoire et pensée religieuse (XXVe semaine de Synthèse)", in *Rev. de Synthèse*, 3rd quartr. 37–39 (1965), pp. 298-9.

mistrust when what is urgently required today is a dialogue for a better understanding of the faith based on the following proposition: the history of dogma is the inventory of the inexhaustible wealth of what is given in revelation because historians should show theologians that the history of dogma is not only a *progressive* but also a *pluralist* understanding of an inexhaustible object: the God-Man in his Mystical Body which the Church is.

2. *History and Exegesis*

To grasp the "mystery" fully, it would probably be necessary to abandon a facile split between sacred history and the history of the Church. Although it may be true that apostolic times represent the *terminus a quo* of the study of Christianity as an historical event, it is none the less true that one cannot ignore its Old Testament roots which arise at every point of the New Covenant, in such a way, moreover, as to feed certain "Catholic biblicist" collective psychologies as in the South of the United States. Whatever one's attitude to an unwarranted extrapolation, historians can renew their own thinking about the event when specialists in Holy Scripture challenge the duality of a profane and a sacred history. Pierre Bockel puts it extremely well: "It is perfectly obvious that in God's eyes there can only be a single history in which his Son Jesus Christ is present so that it may become entirely sacred history. Is not the destiny of the Church, the invisible body of Jesus Christ immersed in time, to be, in the last analysis, the ferment in history enabling it to be lived in its full depth, enabling men to go beyond outward appearances and the mere succession of events to grasp its reality as history of salvation? ... To see in history no more than a dreary succession of events would in effect amount to mistaking man's mere shadow for the real thing ... to affirming the autonomy of the body with regard to the soul, and would constitute open defiance towards the Covenant, the mystery of the incarnation of the Word, the unified person of Christ, the unifying power of the Spirit, the nature of the Church and the prophetic mission."[13]

But because they are dealing with an historical matter already refined by tradition, biblicists are aware that historical exegesis

[13] P. Bockel, "L'Histoire vue d'un seul regard", in *Bible et Terre Sainte*, 53–54 (1963), pp. 5–6.

no longer suffices. Paul Ricoeur remarked at the second conference of the French Catholic Association for Bible Study that historical exegesis certainly discovers the primitive meaning of a text but its analysis already involves an interpretation, a bringing together of two cultures; the scholar is thus in danger of "projecting" himself.[14] This is at any rate true unless the historian endows the scholar with his own techniques for researching into collective mentalities. The confrontation of the exegete's notion of civilization with the historian's would widen the horizons of an overall or "total" history: one only has to think of the advantage to be drawn from those towns famous for their historical deposits; after Memphis and Phebes, Tanis records the tumultuous destiny and the clash of peoples on its territory from the age of the great pyramids to the last of the Ptolemies. To reinterpret the materials discovered in the cross-fire of archaeological, linguistic, historical and exegetical techniques, would be an interesting application of this wider approach to history.[15]

III. Church History as a Pluridisciplinary Instruction in Religious Studies

Here and there in France we are beginning to witness the setting up of interdisciplinary seminaries to train students in religious studies. The National Council for the *ratio studiorum* of the seminaries of the Company of Saint-Sulpice, under the presidency of Mgr Paty, the bishop of Luçon, is following these attempts at renewal closely. They are as yet too fragmentary to produce a doctrine capable of eliciting plans for a general course of instruction covering several disciplines. However, certain teachers who are aware of the changes taking place in Church history admit without any sense of abdication the precariousness surrounding the autonomy of certain "treatises". Their reincorporation into genuinely historical instruction is sought above all for the following:

1. *Borderline Subjects: Apologetics and Ecclesiology*

In so far as it is a science concerned with credibility, apologetics

[14] Cf. *La Croix*, 13 September 1969.
[15] P. Montet, "Tanis", in *Bible et Terre Sainte*, 53–54 (1963), pp. 10–28.

still likes to visualize itself in the theological spectrum as the section responsible for "defence", employing philosophy and history, but in the light of faith. By this token, philosophy and history are utilized merely as supporting sciences for faith or "auxiliaries"[16] because one cannot see what a philosopher would make of the idea of a revelation which was simply possible, that is to say non-contradictory, and what an historian would make of the affirmation of a divine nature possessed in an undivided fashion by the Father and the Son. It is true that there would be a large risk of burdening "human" disciplines with affirmations proper to the realm of faith. But would it not be interesting to show precisely what a *lived* faith has to offer both from the angle of a phenomenology of religions and from the angle of the attitudes of the Christian people towards signs of credibility such as the miracles—and this without encroaching upon the jurisdiction of the specialists? The historian's problem is no longer to adhere to the dogma of consubstantiation but to establish that it moulds a way of thinking and, consequently, to give an account of it so as to throw some sociological light on it for the apologist, going beyond ideological and even doctrinal controversies. The apologist's "defensive" function would then take on a positive quality which has often been found wanting in the past.

The confrontation between historian and theologian would seem even more fruitful in the matter of ecclesiology. Congar has remarked that following the Gregorian reform there was a transition from "an ecclesiology of Christian anthropology to an ecclesiology of the powers, prerogatives and rights of 'the Church', that is to say of the priesthood or hierarchy. The modern treatises *De Ecclesia*, worked out in isolation and for their own sake, are scarcely more than treatises on the Church's public rights."[17] Strong in this degradation, historians have become entrenched in ecclesiastical politics. Thus theologians and historians, for different reasons, emptied the Church of its function as Mystical Body in favour of its social function whereby the Church no longer flaunted its "record" except in reaction against a society or

[16] Y. Congar in an article entitled "Theologie", in *Dict. Théol. Cathol.*, XV, col. 496. Le Bachelet in an article entitled "Apologétique et Apologie", in *Dict. Apolog. Foi Cathol.*, I, col. 190.

[17] Y. Congar, "Ecclesia Mater", in *Vie Spirituelle*, 503 (1964), pp. 324-5.

civilization which had relegated it to a minor position from the eighteenth century onwards. Perhaps because we are so keenly aware nowadays of the need for a political theology, that is to say for the Church to reflect on itself with a view to giving life to its presence in the world, we understand better the necessity for rediscovering this matter of political theology in the very pattern of ecclesiologies.

The historian cannot be unaware of the Church as Mystical Body which founds a hierarchical priesthood of all its members, because that is inherent in the society-Church which he studies. The theologian, on the other hand, must look at the way the Church as bride of Christ becomes incarnate sociologically at different times. Either the two levels are dissociated at the cost of the former and ecclesiology turns into "ecclesiastical politics", or else the complex interplay of the spiritual and the temporal continues to function in the interaction of the two levels and political theology is reached. In collaboration with the theologian, the historian would be able to locate the moments at which these two levels became distorted or joined with one another in the course of centuries. Together they ought to extract from them points of profound significance for our understanding of Christian anthropology.[18]

2. The "Aevum" in Church History

The variety of these confrontations should at least show this: that the Church only rarely assumes in the world the totality and fullness of its functions. Each century or great "moment" of Christianity has a privileged *aevum* followed more or less rapidly by another. Thus the different aspects of the Church are as it were staggered within any one historically homogeneous period. Why, in such a period, is the "time" of pastoral theology or that of spirituality longer and more marked than the "time" of theological reflection? Why is the combination different in another such period? Recording these disparities would be the task of the historian who would then turn to the specialists to help him study the "times" thus singled out and differences in kind.

In restoring them to their place within the long-term view

[18] See B. Plongeron, *op. cit.*, pp. 183–92.

(synchronous vision) one would be better able to perceive the heart-beat of the Christian life in the course of *organic* periods (simultaneous accomplishment of the Church's major functions) and *critical* periods (blossomings, progressions, changes and recessions of the Church's "times"). Turning the diachronisms to good effect would certainly stimulate teaching according to theme.

3. *Teaching according to Theme*

Is this not the ultimate contribution to be made by a pluridisciplinary instruction revolving around history? Without altogether abandoning the traditional divisions into periods, one can conceive of the study of long-term themes: the Church and the faith lived by Christians (Christianization and de-Christianization), the Church in its charitable function (the theology of charity and charitable activities), the problem of religious tolerance from the sixteenth to the twentieth centuries, and so on. . . .

These themes would form the basis for "round table" discussions in which all the specialists concerned, in both the religious and "profane" sciences, would be there alongside the historian. In addition, in the case of more advanced students, these meetings could introduce research into the documents: we have in mind an experimental discussion on the subject of the Christian and death from the seventeenth to the eighteenth centuries. For a term a psychologist, a moralist, a dogmatic theologian and an economist discussed with students the results of their original and enthusiastic analysis of several series of wills discovered by them.

In much the same way, why shouldn't all the different branches of the curriculum converge for a year or so towards a "hot point" of Church history. The topic of Luther, for example, which would involve exegesis and fundamental and sacramental theology as well as ethics and spirituality. . . . There are others!

The educational structures which are everywhere breaking out of their current limitations, and the need for religious studies to check their methodology against the pivotal role of history at the intersection of their different paths, gives us some hope that these few suggestions, however badly formulated they may be, cannot be relegated to Utopia.

Translated by Jonathan Cavanagh

Giuseppe Alberigo

New Frontiers
in Church History

In recent years we have had to revise our opinions about Church
history. First of all, it was a question of re-thinking Christian
origins. It became obvious that our early texts could not be considered merely statically or one-sidedly, or as if they belonged
to an almost mythical past. And when they were demythologized,
viewed as something dynamic and full of diversity, they gave us
an altogether new idea of the early days of Christianity.

It has become quite clear now that we get only a false impression of the facts if we look at the turning-points in the Church's
history from the angle of the winning side. The Council of
Chalcedon and the Monophysite question are a case in point.
It has become a commonplace of Christian thought to dismiss the
losing side at Chalcedon as an unimportant minority, doctrinally
and culturally speaking, unworthy of serious consideration and
having no positive relevance to Christian history.

New perspectives are opened up, likewise, when we drop the
time-honoured habit of centring all our concern on Rome. Our
approach to the Gregorian reform has been very much revised
on this account. Until quite recently, studies on this subject have
confined themselves exclusively to the influence of Rome. But
now, although we can see very well what a centralizing effect
this reform had on the life of the Church, we can see that there
were other areas of influence involved, both in its beginnings and
its development.

Finally, we are in the process of revising our outlook on the
religious history of the sixteenth century, which has until now

been considered essentially in the light of controversy. It will probably take some time to reorientate ourselves here, because some of the points involved are still relevant today. It is not yet possible to think of the sixteenth century from a purely retrospective angle. Modernism is another subject that benefits from a new approach, likewise the development of ecclesiology.

It is evident that historians are beginning to see that they have more problems on their hands besides merely getting their facts right. However, we have only to think of what Dvornik has done to clarify the Photian controversy to realize how basically necessary it is to get things in proportion after they have been systematically confused for centuries by the vast amount that has been written on the subject. To my mind, this is precisely the value of Jedin's work on the Council of Trent, of Lortz on the beginnings of the Reformation in Germany, and of Aubert on the pontificate of Pius IX. These historians have attempted to reconstruct history on a basis of what actually happened, or at least what contemporary accounts claim to have happened. This is a considerable step forward from the kind of historical writing which aims to uphold a thesis and cannot claim to be impartial. I am thinking of Sarpi and Pallavicino on the question of Trent, of Denifle and Grisar and the Protestant apologists for Luther, and all the hagiography and polemics written about Pio Nono.

It is important to realize that such works as these have the positive merit of showing how necessary it is to read historic events in the light of scientific accuracy, for it is comparatively recently that we have stopped reading them purely from the viewpoint of apologetics. Then there is a further problem to overcome, namely the habit of taking only a partial view of these events, and assuming that one aspect of a reality can be considered dominant when it is in fact the result of a prejudice, perhaps cultural, or ideological, or pertaining to a certain kind of ecclesiology.

I propose here to list some of these partial views, in the hope that they may clarify the problems that confront us today—problems which are re-defining the frontiers of Church history.

Normally Church history gives pride of place to orthodoxy, whenever the orthodox position is opposed by whatever seems unorthodox to the Church at the time. The historian must take into account the Church's estimate of unorthodoxy, because it constitutes a fact at a given time, and its influence may have been very far-reaching. But this attitude has always been overlaid by the conviction that an allegiance to orthodoxy is the indispensable condition for an event in the life of the Church to be taken seriously by the historian. It is not by accident that Western Church history has totally neglected the history of the Eastern Churches since the schism. Only the sixteenth-century reformers, having broken with Rome, began to take an interest in Eastern Christianity. Rome had rejected it, as well as them.

Pride of place also went to uniformity, when it was confronted by pluralism. Attitudes of conformity were welcomed, and anything that had to do with specific charisms or an adaptation to singular circumstances was looked down on, because it emphasized difference and nonconformity. In the same way, established attitudes were preferred to new researches, and this has had a very bad effect particularly in the spheres of dogma and spirituality. "Establishment" Christianity was considered preferable to new Christian ventures.

Another privileged position has been that of the clerical contingent as opposed to the laity. Church history has often been reduced to a saga of clerical goings-on, in which the priestly ministry is magnified into something quite out of proportion to its real achievements.

For a number of reasons, including the gradual disappearance of the early Church's eschatological concern, and the influence of Roman law, privilege has been accorded to the Church as an institution. Christian developments that took place on the periphery of the institution, or outside it, have tended to be ignored. This fact has been emphasized in recent years in certain theological and historical currents of the Reformed Churches. By accepting the priority of the institution, Catholic Church history has dwelt upon a multitude of insignificant facts and irrelevant details relating to the institutional Church and its more illustrious members, with the result that most of us know little or nothing of far more influential happenings that did not involve popes and Church dignitaries.[1] And this is the reason why Church history

[1] Eusebius of Caesarea begins his *History of the Church* in a way that is typical of this attitude: "I have decided to write about the successors of the holy apostles during the time which has elapsed since our Saviour's day

seems often to move in fits and starts (they are of course explained by "providence"!). Instead of being visualized as a dynamic development of Christian life, it is seen rather statically as life in terms of institutions—and clearly, life can only be partially expressed in such terms.

To some degree this priority overlaps with another, namely, that of authority in respect to the people who are subject to it. We have only to reflect on the way Church history has always represented the teaching magisterium. Theoretically it has always accepted a magisterium of the people, *in credendo*, but in practice it has ignored it. And here we cannot discount the influence of Graeco-Latin culture in creating all kinds of possibilities for mankind to acquire power over his fellow men, whether it be a matter of property or politics.

Then we come to privileges of a more subtle sort, for instance the priority of one authority over another. You have only to open Denzinger or Mirbt to see how papal authority always has pride of place over councils and synods. Here the Catholic Church is not alone. The Protestants likewise accept the priority of one authority over another. There is a subtle difference, never in fact formulated, but none the less real.

One of the most dangerous priorities, of course, is that of the majority over the minority. Here one must realize that this is not just a distinction between the orthodox and the unorthodox. It happens within the realm of orthodoxy itself. It has the effect of levelling out Church history to the benefit of whoever gets the upper hand, so that minority groups and opinions, which so often express ideas of the greatest value, are dismissed as unimportant.

---

until our own. I shall bring in all the important events in the history of the Church, especially in so far as they concern those who ruled and guided it in its most important centres, preaching and commenting on the Word of God", I, 1, r (*Sources chrétiennes*, 31) (Paris, 1952), 3. We find a curious and significant protest in one of Goethe's Xenien against Church history when it is reduced to a summary of conflicts between institutions, prominent persons, orthodoxy and heresy: "What should I do with Church history?/All I can see is clerics,/How it fares for the Christians, the common people, no one tells me./I could also have said the 'communities', but it would have made no difference./... Church history is nothing more than a mixture of error and force." *Werke*, I (Stuttgart), p. 1122. Cf. also M. de Certeau, "L'histoire religieuse du XVIIe siècle. Problèmes de méthodes", in *Recherches de Science religieuse*, 57 (1969), pp. 231–50.

In fact they often represent traditions and aspirations that are a necessary complement to what has been triumphantly asserted by the majority. This is a point that has some important implications in anthropology and the philosophy of history. To assume that people who get their ideas across have priority over those who do not, is not only untrue, but in Church history it actually makes it impossible to understand certain phenomena that can only be explained in terms of minority views which have not been considered important.[2]

Obviously one accepts canonization as a priority over normal Christian life. But unfortunately there have been historians who have built up the figure of a particular saint to symbolize a whole epoch. We may reasonably ask, therefore, just how far Christian life at a given period can be supposed to have been incarnated in the life of one person, or group of persons. Is this not, perhaps, the fault of a certain kind of historian who must indulge his penchant for heroes and supermen?

Finally we come to the most unacceptable privilege of all, and one that has been far-reaching in its effects—namely, the primacy of West over East. Church history has consistently put the Eastern Churches in a subordinate position, although admittedly it has considered the Greek Church more respectable than the communions of Asia and Africa—Syrians, Copts and so forth. It is this attitude that has brought about our almost total ignorance of Christianity as lived and experienced by these people. For the same reason, we are often unaware that certain events in our own history are ultimately to be explained by the activity of the Eastern Church.

Often, of course, there have been objections raised to such a one-sided view. Gottfried Arnold, K. S. Latourette, E. Benz and various Protestant scholars have maintained the inadequacy of any Church history that lines itself up exclusively with any single confession of the Christian faith.[3] But we know very well that

[2] By this I do not mean to suggest that Church history should concern itself with the kind of Church that might evolve at some future time, and as such is a matter of fantasy. But I do feel that we have to overcome any tendency to identify the Church in itself with any current institution, and for that matter with any current theology.

[3] G. Arnold, *Unparteiische Kirchen- und Ketzerhistorie. Vom Anfang des Neuen Testaments bis auf das Jahr Christi 1688* (Frankfurt, 1729—

this sort of proposition has made very little headway, and can suggest two possible reasons. In the first place, public opinion has been slow to assimilate the ecumenical intention that lies at the root of any such reorientation. In the second place, this ecumenical motivation was itself not really up to the mark when it came to a definite re-thinking of Church history as a scientific discipline.

The ecumenical awareness of Christians is an important development in itself, but it is not the same thing as the history of the Church as it develops along ecumenical lines. It is the confusion of these two distinct developments which leads to the unsatisfactory kind of reconstruction of historic events in which we are all too aware of things having been watered-down in the name of ecumenism. One thing becomes very evident, and that is that you cannot use ecumenism (which is one particular orientation in the Church) as a method of procedure in this science (Church history).[4]

Our foremost Church historians have made us aware of a problem similar to this one, when they maintain that the concept of the Church is rapidly changing in the minds of thinking Christians, and that, as a result, the status of Church history must likewise change. While remaining an historical discipline, it is

---

Hildesheim, 1967); K. S. Latourette, *History of Expansion of Christianity* (New York, 1937–1945); E. Benz, *Kirchengeschichte in Ökumenischer Sicht* (Leiden, 1961). In connection with G. Arnold's book, see P. Meinhold, *Geschichte der kirchlichen Historiographie* (Vienna, 1960), pp. 83–4. On Latourette, see D. Sella, *Gli studi di storia religiosa negli Stati Uniti e l'opera di K. S. Latourette* (Florence, 1958). The search for a new direction is the subject of an article by E. G. Leonard, "Necessité et directives d'une conception nouvelle de l'histoire de l'Eglise", in *Etudes de théologie et d'action évangéliques de la Fac. libre de théologie protestante d'Aix en Provence*, 2 (1941), pp. 119–40.

[4] D. Cantimori has repeatedly pointed out these limits with some clarity in *Studi di storia* (Turin, 1959), pp. 479–80, 483–4, 544, and *Prospettive di storia ereticale italiana del Cinquecento* (Bari, 1960), p. 7. K. E. Skydsgaard, in his essay *La Réformation en tant qu'événement œcuménique*, makes a rigorous distinction of great interest between Church history and its theological interpretation. He shows that Catholics and Protestants alike have been in the habit of seeing the Reformation as something absolutely definitive (p. 242) and adds that polemics and ecumenism can equally reflect mutual indifference and a complete lack of contact. (*Œcumenica*, 1969, pp. 230–50.)

taking on more of the characteristics that classify it under theology. It would seem, therefore, that all the re-thinking that is going on among Christians is bound to affect the way we look at Church history, and make us subject it to the most searching examination.[5]

I must admit, for my part, that I do not share this opinion. I am quite convinced that current Christian thinking is going to affect the whole context, the whole perspective that Church historians have to deal with. And it is precisely because of this that I feel we must be very careful to avoid arbitrary and hasty modifications in the basic structure of a science like Church history. It is a science that has to be definite and solidly based if it is to be of real use in the Christian outlook of today.

Church history is, and should remain, properly historical. It has its own object, its own proper mode of treating that object, and it has its own method. The object in question is the Church, and therefore all the Christian Churches. We have to think of the Church, not in a dogmatic but in a phenomenological sense. Every manifestation of life, of thought, of organization is involved, in so far as it has come about with a specific reference to Christianity. The status of Christianity is ecclesial, and there is a wide range of meanings to be explored in that word, according to different periods and differing tendencies. It is quite evident that we cannot take seriously any exclusive interpretation of the word. The object of Church history cannot be simply "the true Church", any more than it can be a purely spiritual and invisible Church. Nor can we limit the concept to a Church expressed merely institutionally, in terms of what has received legal sanction. The object of Church history is not the plan of salvation either, for this involves the history of all creation, nor is it the anticipation of the Kingdom which we believe to be present in the life of the Church.

[5] R. Aubert, General Introduction to Nouvelle histoire de l'Eglise, I (Paris, 1963), pp. 7–26. H. Jedin, "Kirchengeschichte als Heilsgeschichte?", in Saeculum, 5 (1954), pp. 119–28; Kirche des Glaubens—Kirche der Geschichte, I (Freiburg, 1966), pp. 37–48; "Kirchengeschichte", in L.Th.K., 6 (²1961), cols. 209–11; the introduction to Handbook of Church History, I (London & New York, 1965). La storia della Chiesa è teologia e storia (Milan, 1968). C. W. Dugmore, Ecclesiastical History. No Soft Option (London, 1959).

The perspective in which Church history studies the Church is the succession of what is visibly manifested in the course of time. Sources are consulted for the phenomena they deal with, not for evidence of the working of divine providence. Thus, Church history does not appear to be in any sense classifiable as a theological discipline, at least not in so far as theology implies that we must always begin with the data of revelation, or revelation as such, wherever and however we find it. Christianity and the Church are the object of theology, but theology approaches them in a way which is qualitatively different from the approach of Church history. We can say in regard to the Church, as we can say about creation, that it goes back to a unique act of God, but as far as we are concerned it has to be conceived in various different ways.

The methods that Church history uses are, naturally enough, historical methods. These imply a critical analysis of sources that is essentially positive and empirical. This kind of method can never possibly reveal completely the complex structure of the Church as something human and at the same time divine. This brings us back to the problem that we find in almost any science, namely the connection between positive research and the complex structures which are the object of research. To try to evade this limitation in the study of Church history would be simply foolish. Far from bringing about any improvement, it would only be a step backwards. The usefulness of Church history depends greatly on the scientific accuracy that goes into its research. We can only bring out all the possibilities of the subject by being aware of its true nature as a science, and accepting its limitations. If we can accept this, we can reasonably dismiss any attempt that is made to give Church history a status and a scope which do not belong to it. Here I am thinking particularly of the sort of work in which the historian takes a too specialized view of the *preambula fidei*, or confuses historical reality with the mystery of salvation, or speaks from the standpoint of a certain period in the history of the Church's thought.[6] When we can accept that Church history

[6] The question whether or not faith is required in a Church historian has been tackled by R. Aubert in his "Historiens croyants et historiens incroyants devant l'histoire religieuse", in *Recherches et debats*, 47 (1964), pp. 28-43.

is a science it will at last be able to cope adequately with its
subject-matter, and get over the positivistic phase at every level of
research.

From this point of view, history has made great progress in
our time. Church history is still somewhat uncertain in following
the same lines. Many historians still have an instinctive mistrust
in their attitude, and much discussion of the *habitus fidei* and of
the theological nature of Church history has not been a good influence. But, in fact, the fullest possibilities of Church history can
be realized if only we will relate our subject-matter to the improved methods which have been perfected in the study of history
in general. From the study of history as something partial and
purely factual (*événementielle*) we can move on to a global conception. We can reconstruct an historical event by studying all
the factors that brought it about, or in any sense related to it at
the time. In this way we can, for instance, dismiss the overriding
importance once attributed to political and diplomatic history.
We can arrive at a truer evaluation of the part that society plays
in history. We can appreciate the way in which different aspects
of reality cohere. We can integrate various elements—psychological, doctrinal and spiritual—which historical positivism has often
tended to shun.

Historical research, it must be admitted, has not progressed
qualitatively a great deal above the level it had when it was first
accepted as a science. Progress here depends largely on a radical
reformulation of our ideas of time, visibility, and so forth.

Having summarized these various points, I should like now to
go on to an outline of what I think of as a unifying approach to
a particular period. The sixteenth century is a particularly dra-
matic one from a Christian point of view, and, what is more,
it still has a certain effect on historical research in our time. It
places some very narrow limits on our knowledge of events.
Ecumenism, and some of the re-thinking that has gone on in
ecclesiology, have had only a peripheral effect, and have sometimes even produced positive confusion.

Things happened to the Church in the sixteenth century which
affected Christianity profoundly, introducing totally new elements, which took root so quickly that we think of them now as

perfectly natural categories in Western culture. We have only to think, for example, of how quickly the Roman obedience and the Reformed Church took on the name of "religion".[7] For such reasons as this, we must be careful not to substitute our present-day outlook for the outlook of that period. We must accept it for the reality that it is. We must be careful not to iron out or in any sense minimize the tensions, the ruptures, the intolerances, the responsibilities and the abuses—everything in fact that is involved in this conflict between two sides, each claiming to be legitimately Christian, and each denying the claims of its opponent. There is no room here for well-meaning denials of clerical corruption, or the exposition of Luther's unconscious motives, or the refusal to admit that the ninety-five theses were ever nailed up.[8] What we are trying to discover is a global, unifying vision of what Christians and their Churches were actually achieving in the life of sixteenth-century Europe.

If we have the courage to follow this line with all our critical wits about us, we shall get some really interesting results. We shall in fact arrive at a much more satisfactory view of religious life in the sixteenth century. A vast area of history is waiting to be recovered, involving all the convictions, the behaviour and the attitudes which are common to all Christians. The institutional side of Christianity, and the intolerance of both Catholics and Protestants, have effectively managed to conceal so much of all this from the attention of historians. There is more here than the opposition of two Christian persuasions, and the break-up of

---

[7] The formula *cujus regio ejus religio*, attributed to the Protestant canonist Joachim Stephani, finalizes a trend in the thinking of the time. An analysis of the texts in the *Confessio Augustana* (1530), of the treaty of Augusta (1555) and the treaty of Westphalia (1648) shows a progressive modification. *Religio* in 1530 meant the whole of Western Christianity. In 1555, "religion" is already identified with "confession": *bede Religionen, alte Religion oder Augspurgische Confession*. By 1648, the expression *utraque religione* is commonly used. Cf. J. Heckel, "Cura religionis—Ius in sacra—Ius circa sacra", in *Festschrift für U. Stutz* (Stuttgart, 1938), pp. 224–98. Finally the *Codex iuris canonici* lays down the law for cases of "mixed religion".

[8] E. Iserloh, *Luther zwischen Reform und Reformation. Der Thesenanschlag fand nicht statt* (Münster, 1966). R. Baumer, "Die Diskussion um Luthers Thesenanschlag. Forschungergebnisse und Forschungsaufgaben", in *Um Reform und Reformation* (Münster, 1968), pp. 53–95.

faith (*Die Glaubensspaltung*). There is, in fact, a communion in the same faith, the awareness of belonging to the same reality, and of sharing the same destiny. If we concentrate on the division between Catholics and Protestants, naturally enough we get two Church histories, and sometimes more, instead of a single one. There is the history of the Catholic Church, the history of the Reformed Churches, the history of the Anabaptists or the anti-Trinitarians. But we can get over this obstacle once we have accepted the idea of a global history, which we find already accepted in the world of historical research. There have been some moves in this direction,[9] but what we need is to be systematically orientated towards the idea.

It is in this dimension that we immediately feel the need to re-integrate the history of the Eastern Churches, especially, although not exclusively, the Greek and Russian Churches. Recent historical studies have all too often neglected this vital area, or treated it merely marginally. This has had the effect of obscuring some very important links between Eastern and Western Churches, which continued to exist for a time after the Council of Florence. It has also neglected to consider the great Westward emigration that followed the fall of Constantinople.[10] Again, very little is known about the state of Christianity under Moslem domination, and its links with Christian life in the West.

Another point deserving more thorough examination is the significance for the sixteenth-century Church of those Christians who found themselves excluded alike by Catholics and Reformers. These are very important people because they managed to uphold

[9] H. Jedin, "Ein 'Turmerlebnis' des jungen Contarini", in *Historisches Jahrbuch*, 70 (1951), pp. 115–30. In this article Jedin emphasizes the parallel between the spiritual experience of the future Cardinal Contarini and that of the Augustinian Martin Luther. J. Lebrun, "Le christianisme et les hommes à la fin du 16 siècle", in *Nouvelle Histoire de l'Eglise*, III (Paris, 1968, pp. 232–54. Lebrun here attempts a global approach in dealing with a short space of time.

[10] In recent manuals of Church history and the history of spirituality, authors who are aware of the problem usually give a chapter, or at least an appendix, dealing with Eastern Christianity. This had already been done by A. Fliche and V. Martin. Such good intentions and ecumenical approaches as these only make it more obvious that such a procedure is inadequate from the point of view of writing history.

the evangelical ideal of non-violence in a period that had no time for it.

Christianity in the sixteenth century still had some interesting connections with the Jews and the Moslems. It only requires the effort to get over certain political and psychological barriers to appreciate this fact.

In order to broaden our knowledge of the common life of Christians, it would help greatly if research were done on the history of lay confraternities, on knowledge of the Bible and works of piety in this period, and the approach to the sacraments and to worship in general. It is in this field that we get the clearest picture of religious life in its economic and social context. And this does not in any sense minimize what are properly religious motives in the lives of Christians and their Churches. It simply helps us to see that the religious struggles of the time took place between real men, and not angels, thoroughly conditioned by and involved in their social, economic and political environment.[11]

A global history of religious life in the sixteenth century has to treat the study of controversy in such a way as to unify schools of thought which set themselves up as opponents to each other. As a typical example we can take Baronius and his group in Rome, and the authors of the "Centuries of Magdeburg". They took different sides, but none the less were united by the fact that they were facing exactly the same problems. And there are many aspects of Christian culture that would benefit by the kind of study which not only compares but seeks to unify opposing currents. Instead of treating these as perpetually antagonistic monads, we can approach them as relating to one and the same Christian reality.

Even within the principal Churches—Roman, Lutheran and Calvinist—Church history has generally been limited, even exclusively tied down, to the history of a current of thinking that

[11] Only one aspect of this vast problem has been treated in depth, namely the influence of Calvinism in social progress (Max Weber). Here we may ask if there are not two *a priori* judgments at work in the minds of historians. They tend to see the influence of religion on the welfare of nations as a weapon of apologetics, and they sometimes take a too negative view of the break-up of the Reformation, which can colour their judgment of its social and economic consequences.

has successfully set itself up as a hegemony. However, in a period of intense activity and profound change, we cannot overlook the activities of the minority, since they played an important part with respect to the successful majority. The minority started up new and often far-reaching ideas, and unless we have some appreciation of these we can have only a partial view of the truth about Christianity in this period.

These are only a few of the integrations that will have to be made in the sphere of sixteenth-century religious life. There are probably many others that will come to light when we concentrate on what was held in common by the differing factions.

Certain judgments which were formulated in the sixteenth century have been inherited by successive generations of historians, and have continued to perpetuate rigid classifications which now need to be overhauled. Let us take, for instance, the idea of justification as propounded by the Church of Rome and the Reformers. Rome, Wittenberg and Geneva found their opponents' theses irreconcilable with their own, notably in their discussions at Ratisbon. Today, however, researches such as those of Hans Küng on justification show that the various positions are by no means irreconcilable. This is made possible by the fact that we have wider perspectives and a more developed theology than were available in the sixteenth century. This does not in any way minimize the fact that at that time the disagreements involved seemed insoluble. It simply emphasizes the fact that our knowledge of history has broadened out, and it would be irrelevant to accept *a priori* the limits imposed by sixteenth-century polemics.

Another period judgment which is being radically reviewed concerns the hostility aimed at humanism as if it were something anti-Christian. Church history has systematically neglected the work of Erasmus, and likewise of almost anyone else who has lived and worked in a Christian context and in one way or another made a specifically humanist contribution to it.[12]

A final example, and a very interesting one, is the importance

[12] A. Weiler, "Scholasticism and the Christian Humanism of the Renaissance", in *Concilium* (September 1967), pp. 16–24 (American edn. vol. 27). For the significance of Machiavelli, cf. D. Cantimori, "Nicolò Machiavelli, il politico e lo storico", in *Storia della letteratura italiana*, IV (Milan, 1966), pp. 7–53.

given to what is known as *theologische Unklarheit*, first of all by Catholic theologians dealing with controversy, and recently taken up again by Lortz. This theological uncertainty is considered an essentially negative factor in the break-up of the sixteenth century.[13] In fact, this approach would seem to imply the rejection of pluralism, with pride of place given to what is absolutely certain, and a preference invariably shown towards the monolithic structure, despite the existence of many different formulations of doctrine. It shows an attitude mistrustful of research, and a willingness to overlook the fact that the first fifteen centuries of the Church's history show considerable evidence of pluralism. We can ask ourselves precisely how much this attitude owes to real historical research, and how much to *a priori* judgments dictated by convictions that have nothing to do with research.

It is useful to point out, in this context, that the history of the Church in the sixteenth century can furnish materials for a rethinking of the overall significance of religious events going on in Europe at the time. This is all too often presented as something negative, as if it meant nothing more than separation, and the end of religious unity. A careful historical examination will reveal, precisely in the ruptures involved, a whole series of positive results from which present-day Christianity has benefited. But it needs courage and clear thinking to make such an admission. The sixteenth century witnessed an upsurge of ideas, events and new kinds of experience which contributed much that was of value. We have only to think, for instance, of the new importance given to the laity, or rather the universal priesthood of all the faithful. Then there is the fact that the laity made their first real contact with Scripture, and a great deal of energy was liberated, preparing the way for the missionary expansion that was to follow. In theology we can see the positive value of pluralism in the formulation of doctrine, in the patterns of religious life and the ecclesiastical set-up.

Such considerations as these do not directly concern Church history perhaps, but they are the kind of useful contribution that Church history can make when it really gets to grips with its subject.

[13] J. Lortz, *Die Reformation in Deutschland*, I (Freiburg, [2]1948), pp. 137-8.

6—c.

I would like to conclude by suggesting that when Church history aligns itself to the new frontiers adopted by historical research, it will be able to produce some far-reaching modifications in our knowledge of Christianity as it was lived in the sixteenth century, and in every other period.

However, I hardly feel I can leave the matter here, on account of questions that still remain open for discussion, questions of which we shall be all the more aware if we adopt the approach of historical research in the field of Church history.

Quite obviously we must anticipate a certain tension here, because on the one hand the subject of Church history is the Church, in the widest sense of the term, and on the other hand we are looking for a global dimension in the treatment of our subject. The meaning that Church historians put into the word "Church" depends on what they get out of the sources of the period they are studying.[14] This always means that a large cross-section of Christians is left out. But if we drop the word "Church" and substitute for it "Christianity", "missionary expansion" or "preaching the Gospel", we leave the way open to an approach that lacks definition, and could land Church history in an ambiguous position somewhere between history in the strict sense, and a theology of history, or history of salvation.[15] This, I feel, would be a backward step.

[14] It is a common opinion among Catholic scholars that the approach of Church history should be guided by theology. Cf. H. Dickerhof, "Kirchenbegriff Wissenschaftentwicklung, Bildungssoziologie und die Formen kirchlicher Historiographie", in *Historisches Jahrbuch*, 89 (1969), pp. 176–202. G. Denzler, "Kirchengeschichte im Lichte der Wahrheit", in *Abschied von Trient. Theologie am Ende des Kirchlichen Mittelalters*, ed. J. Bielmeier (Regensburg, 1969), p. 99. J. Wodka has attempted to set out the ecclesiastical norms for the guidance of Church historians in his "Mistero della Chiesa nella prospettiva della storia ecclesiastica", in *Il mistero della Chiesa*, I (Rome, 1966), pp. 581–786. I have reserves about the validity of his approach, and cannot, in any case, accept that theology should be allowed to determine the actual procedure of historical research.

[15] G. Ebeling, *Kirchengeschichte als Geschichte der Auslegung der Hl. Schrift* (Tübingen, 1947)—reprinted in *Wort Gottes und Tradition* (Göttingen, 1964), pp. 9–27. H. Bornkamm, *Grundgriss zum Studium der Kirchengeschichte* (Gütersloh, 1949), p. 17. H. Karpp, "Kirchengeschichte als theologische Disziplin", in *Festschrift R. Bultmann* (Stuttgart, 1949), pp. 149–67. For these authors, Church history has a wider scope than it has

Another open question concerns the influence that might be exercised on the scientific status of Church history by the emergence of "underground" Churches, which emphasize the existence of the sacred in society. Church history in our time, and certainly in the future, will have to take account of this new phenomenon, and perfect some technique for maintaining a balance between the different scales involved.

This is already to some extent required if we are not to make the mistake of identifying our "global" history of the Church with that of the universal Church. If it is evident that we have to develop a global history of the universal Church, it is even more urgent that we try to cast some light on the global history of local Churches and communities. No Church historian can ignore the new importance of concrete Christian communities both on the existential level and the ecclesiological. This is something that belongs to a much bigger dialectic of communion with other Churches and communities. It implies not only a new stage in the writing of Church history, but also a safeguard against our wider approach to Church history resolving itself yet into something purely Western or European.

Finally there is a rather delicate problem yet to be resolved, about the kind of anthropology that is needed to underpin the kind of Church history we have been talking about. Historians of the Church will have to examine more closely, not only ecclesiology, but their actual conception of what man really is, and, above all, their formulation of working hypotheses and their sorting out of priorities on this basis. We have only to think of the

---

for those writers who concentrate on its juridical and institutional aspects, and they try to overcome the limiting fixation with what is visible in the Church, when it comes to historical research. It does not in fact appear that the various alternatives have a sufficiently concrete character to determine a definite line of research. But if we conscientiously use the methods of historical research as they are generally understood, there is no doubt that we can rediscover much that traditional Church history has preferred to overlook.

From another point of view, Karpp's desire to remove Church history from the auxiliary position assigned to it by K. Barth seems reasonable enough, but it does not seem realistic as long as Church history is given a theological status. This can only be done by insisting on the fact that it is primarily an historical pursuit, and an autonomous one, even though theology and Church history are interdependent.

comparatively short space of time it took the early Church to re-orientate its eschatology as soon as it became evident that the advent of the kingdom was still remote. Whether or not an historian pursues his researches in this direction depends on his faith and on the convictions he owes to his culture.

I will admit quite frankly that the approach I have outlined implies a full acceptance of the secularization of Church history, as long as we understand by this term a serious acceptance of history as a science with its own scientific method. It is a secularization that is neither positivist nor anti-clerical. It will have to overcome denominational barriers, and reject any temptation to be pseudo-theological. An "open" secularization of Church history will consider scientifically the different form of Christian life that have succeeded one another in the course of time—forms which, for a believer, are "signs", to be read by the theologian in the light of God's revealed plan of salvation.

We need have no illusions about objective history or completely detached historians, but on the other hand it is vital that Church history should establish its status as an historical discipline, with everything that that implies today. I feel sure that this would bring about quite a new kind of Church history, and that we would finally overcome our temptation to see the Church always and exclusively in its visible aspect.

Translated by Geoffrey Webb

Yves Congar

Church History as a
Branch of Theology

ONE could dispute the meaning of each one of the component
parts of the title of this article but especially the width of meaning
to be given to the word "Church". Increasingly it is being taken
to mean "people of God", and included under the heading of
the history of this people is that of the Christian bodies not in
communion with Rome. Occasionally one hears references to the
"history of Christianity".... As for the expression "branch of
theology" (*locus theologicus*), it is used here roughly in the sense
in which it was used by Melchior Cano (1562), who merits attention in this context for his remark that theologians whose theories
left history out of account ought to be considered uneducated and
coarse.[1] The "branches", or *loci*, denote the different sources of
theological knowledge, worked out according to theological
criteria.

In one sense the history of the Church includes everything,
even, in its widest sense, the Scriptures themselves. It includes
ancient epigraphy and iconography, the liturgies and the *praxis
Ecclesiae* often invoked by St Thomas in sacramentary theology,
the writings of the Fathers and of theologians, the documents
issued by councils and popes, the lives of the saints, and so on.
These diverse factors do not concern us here: they are dealt with
as separate chapters in the manuals entitled *De locis*. There they
are studied almost exclusively from the point of view of their
content, which the authors attempt to define in an unbelievably

---

[1] *De locis theologicis*, XI, c. 2, §3: *Opera* (Padua, 1714), pp. 271-2.

legalistic fashion.[2] Basically these manuals show no interest in the historicity, as such, of these various factors, except when it serves the authors' apologetical purpose to stress their antiquity value. Apart from that, the fact that they belong to a specific time and place hardly counts. We, on the other hand, are here very much concerned with the fact that something new and different happened, was thought or was said at such and such a time and in such and such a place, in relation to specific data both before and after. In short, it is the historical as such which interests us. Or rather, knowledge of the historical, of what happened at different times and in different places. How does this knowledge affect what the theologian does?

I. THE PART PLAYED BY A KNOWLEDGE OF HISTORY

It is now a cliché to say that Christianity, following and along with the Jewish religion, is essentially historical. God has made himself known in deeds which his people recall, and interpret in faith, and to which words and inspired writings have given the full force of revelation. Since the beginnings of historical and biblical criticism, theology has had to face the problem of the relation or connection between the affirmations of faith and the data open to reasonable historical criticism. This has been the problem of Protestant theology since the beginning of the nineteenth century. It lay behind the modernist crisis in the Catholic Church. Since Rudolf Bultmann it has taken a new form and acquired renewed force. From now on any theology which does not reckon with it, especially in Christology, cannot hope to be of interest to anyone really informed. What is more, all the plans for reforming clerical studies, and even the conciliar decree *Optatam totius*, art. 16, favour an approach to dogmatic questions via their development on the biblical, patristic, historical levels (through "the history of dogma and its relationship to the general history of the Church"). Henceforth any theology which fails to contain both a discussion of the origins and development, and an historical and reasonably critical treatment, of the documents of Scripture will be deemed inadequate.

[2] J. M. Levasseur does the same thing in *Le lieu théologique "Histoire"* (1960).

The problem of the evolution or development of dogma has been with us since the last century. Whereas Vatican I was hardly aware of it, Vatican II recognized it (*Dei verbum*, art. 8); but at a time when it had already been reformulated in the thinking of informed theologians. Improved and more critical understanding of the real facts, and a more rigorous realization of the historicity and conditioning of theological and even dogmatic formulations by the problems and cultural resources of a particular time, no longer permitted such a simple, optimistic view of history: history was understood less as a continual process of "development", that is as a progress achieved through a gradual unfolding of what was already implicit, and more as a series of formulations of the one content of faith diversifying and finding expression in different cultural contexts.[3]

Originally, history had been expected to defend and illustrate Catholic standpoints. It was necessary in the sixteenth century.[4] That much remains valid. Pius XII did not restrict the usefulness of positive theology simply to that but took up once again Pius IX's idea of theology serving to show how doctrine defined by "the Church" is contained in the sources.[5] Clearly it must do more than this. We have become more aware of the historical conditioning of the documents of the magisterium itself—with regard to language, mental categories, a framework of concerns affecting the whole approach to certain questions. An entire historical hermeneutic is called for in relation to conciliar documents, and to those of the ordinary magisterium, popes and others in authority.[6] We should need a philological, historical and

[3] See, in this connection, E. Schillebeeckx, *Théologie d'aujourd'hui et de demain* (a lecture given in Chicago) (Paris, 1967), pp. 121–37; J.-P. Jossua, "Immobilité, progrès ou structurations multiples des doctrines chrétiennes?', in *Revue des Sciences philosophiques et théologiques*, 52 (1968), pp. 173–200; M. Seckler, "Der Fortschrittgedanke in der Theologie", in *Theologie im Wandel* (Tübingen, 1967), pp. 41–67. In a different context, Gregory Baum speaks of the "re-focusing of the Gospel ... a new response to God's Word in a new age", in *The Credibility of the Church Today*, A Reply to Charles Davis (London, 1968), p. 152.

[4] Cano, *op. cit.*, XI, c. 2 §4 (273b); P. Polman, *L'élément historique dans la Controverse religieuse du XVIe siècle* (Gembloux, 1932).

[5] The encyclical *Humani generis* (12 August 1950): DSch 3886.

[6] Some suggestive comments are made by P. Fransen, *Problèmes de l'autorité* (*Unam Sanctam*, 38) (Paris, 1962), pp. 93–100.

canonical commentary on *Denzinger*. Nothing less could restore the exact meaning and force of the texts. Pius IX's *Syllabus* is only honestly to be understood in terms of the historical, and in large part the Italian, context in which it was written; the documents referred to in this list are full of allusions to the social and political scene in Europe.

At the present time, honest recognition of the historicity and to some extent the relativity of many acts, texts and attitudes is the best form of apologetics. The difficulty, frequently described by Hans Küng and rendered more acute by actions such as that taken by Charles Davis, is for the Church to be credible, trustworthy. For it to be this—as is its duty quite apart from any consideration of "utility"—it should get rid of numerous fictions which clutter it, and lift taboos which have fallen into disuse and are anyway unacceptable to intelligent people.[7]

Knowledge of history makes possible a healthy relativism, which is quite different from scepticism. Relativism is, on the contrary, a way of being and seeing oneself more truly, and by perceiving the relativity of that which really is relative, it is a way of attributing absoluteness only to what really is absolute. Thanks to history we take proper stock of things, we avoid the mistake of taking for "tradition" that which is only recent and which has altered more than once in the course of time. History helps us to avoid over-dramatizing anxieties aroused in us with evil consequences by new ideas and forms. If by history we mean more than mere erudition and journalistic reporting on the past, it can help us find our true place in the present, become more aware of what really is at stake and the meaning of the tensions we experience.[8] From this angle, contemporary history and what the Germans call *Zeitgeschichte*, a discipline which is making remarkable progress alongside religious sociology, are bearing

---

[7] H. Kühner, *Tabus der Kirchengeschichte* (Zürich, 1963).

[8] Within his own perspective, which this author does not share, Marx wrote as a young man: "The reform of consciousness consists solely in making the world aware of its consciousness... in explaining its own actions to it (...) Thus we can sum up the aim of our periodical in a single phrase: self-understanding: *Selbstverständigung....*" *Deutsch-Französische Jahrbücher*, February 1844. Letter to Ruge of September 1843.

much fruit.[9] Mention must also be made of the historical study of history, which is not at all a sort of attempt to outbid erudite research but an excellent means of self-criticism revealing how, and due to what pressures, men and events in the past have been misinterpreted. Luther is a case in point.[10] Knowledge of the past, used as a means of situating ourselves better in the present, can help us plan the future. Teilhard de Chardin used to say: "The past has revealed to me the construction of the future."[11] This seems obviously true as far as the history of ecclesiology goes. Knowledge of this history elucidates the work of Vatican II and the direction in which things are moving.

There is one area in which the salutary effect of history has already been and must continue to be demonstrably and exceptionally fruitful, namely ecumenism. Speaking quite generally, H. I. Marrou has pointed to the cathartic value of historical awareness as a liberation from the burden of the past.[12] For centuries, with inadequate knowledge both of history and of the

[9] Cf. B. Stasiewski, "Kirchengeschichte und Zeitgeschichte", in *Reformata reformandu, Festg. H. Jedin* (Münster, 1965), vol. II, pp. 631–44; V. Conzemius, "The Necessity of Scientific Contemporary Church History", in *Concilium* (September 1966), pp. 9–22 (American edn., vol. 17).

[10] Concerning Luther, see A. Herte, *Das katholische Lutherbild im Bann der Lutherkommentare des Cochläus*, 3 vols. (Münster, 1943); my own article "Luther vu par les catholiques ou de l'utilité de faire l'histoire de l'histoire", in *Revue des Sciences philosophiques et théologiques*, 34 (1950), pp. 507–18. Since then there have been numerous assessments: T. Sartory in *Una Sancta*, 16 (1961), pp. 38–54, 186–97; A. Ahlbrecht, *ibid.*, 18 (1963), pp. 174–83; R. Stauffer, *Le catholicisme à la découverte de Luther* (Neuchâtel, 1966); F. W. Kantzenbach in *Lutheran World*, 13 (1966), pp. 255–72; H. Jedin in *Chicago Studies*, 5 (1966), pp. 53–63; A. Brandenburg, *Katholische Lutherstudien* (Paderborn, 1966); E. Iserloh in *Concilium* (April 1966), pp. 4–15 (American edn., vol. 14); A. Hasler, *Luther in der katholischen Dogmatik* (Munich, 1968).

Similar work has been done on Photius by F. Dvornik, *Le schisme de Photius* (Paris, 1950).

[11] *Lettres de voyage (1923–1939)* (Paris, 1956), p. 186.

[12] H. I. Marrou, *De la connaissance historique* (Paris, 1954), pp. 273 f.: "Historical awareness brings about a true catharsis, a liberation of our sociological unconscious, somewhat similar to the liberation sought after by psychoanalysts on the psychological plane ... there seems to exist, in all seriousness, a parallel here: in both cases we note the (at first sight) surprising mechanism whereby 'knowledge of the past cause modifies the present state of affairs'; in both cases man frees himself from the past which until then had weighed obscurely on him, not by forgetting it but by striving to recapture it, to take it on himself in full consciousness so

diversity of local situations, people have judged and anathe-
matized each other without a thought for the validity of anyone
else's point of view. People believed that the views they themselves held had always been held. There was no sense of perspective. One sought to convert the opposite viewpoint to one's own.
Historical knowledge has permitted files on several controversial
matters to be reopened; the case of the so-called *monophysitism*
of the pre-Chalcedonians;[13] the case of the patriarch Photius
(F. Dvornik); the case of the excommunications of 1054; the case
of the Jansenist schism in Utrecht.[14] Luther has already been
mentioned. History has also opened up topics previously obscured
by controversy, for example the subject of tradition.[15] We are beginning to experience this catharsis, this liberation through history towards a wider truth. It is my own personal experience that
every time (or practically every time) that I have gone back to the
original facts and documents I discovered something different
from what I had been led to believe.

II. THE EPISTEMOLOGICAL AND THEOLOGICAL ASPECTS

Historians will permit a would-be theologian to pose a question
of principle. It is this. We admit that theology is the systematic
elaboration of what has been revealed, yet we state that revelation
had ceased by the end of the apostolic era, at least in the sense
which has been well expressed by Henri de Lubac, that it attained
its fullness and culmination when the testimony concerning Christ
had been borne. As St John of the Cross says: "God has nothing
more to tell us since what he once declared in separate utterances
through the prophets he has now said definitively by giving us the

---

as to integrate it. This is the meaning of the assertion so often made from
Goethe to Dilthey and Croce that historical knowledge frees man from the
weight of the past. Here once again history appears as a source of instruction, the instrument and sphere of our freedom."

[13] Pius XII, the encyclical *Sempiternus rex* (8 September 1951): *AAS*, 43
(1951), pp. 636–7.
[14] Declaration of the mixed working group between representatives of
the Roman Catholic Church and the Jansenist Church of Utrecht (7 November 1966). Text given in English in *One in Christ*, 3 (1967), pp. 216–18.
[15] The American contingent which studied this question for the Conference on Faith and Order held in Montreal (1963) made this point on
several occasions.

whole in his Son."[16] So is everything already settled? Will eschatology, as Karl Barth once said, consist merely of that moment
when the cover is taken off the table which has been laid since
time began? Does history bring nothing new?

Such a view would raise at least three objections which are
perhaps three ways of putting the same difficulty: (1) the objection based on the truth of history which is the sphere in which
we exercise our freedoms; this includes the notion of novelty, of
the production of the still-to-come. (2) The objection based on
the biblical notion of time frequently highlighted during the past
twenty years and described by Claude Tresmontant as follows:
"In biblical thought, as in the works of Bergson, eternity co-
exists with a time of creation and invention. Time is not the unfolding of that which was already settled out of time in such a
way that someone looking from within the temporal sphere could
have foreseen at a glance what had been settled once and for all
(unless, of course, we are talking about God...). Time is really
perpetual genesis of 'unforeseeable novelty'."[17] It has been per-
ceptively pointed out that in the Odyssey Ulysses returns to the
point from which he started, Ithaca, whereas biblical history is
concerned with obedience to the injunction to go forth, to go
forward: Abraham, the Exodus, the Gospel as "passage" and call
to go continually beyond. (3) The third objection is contained
in a critical study of *Gaudium et spes*, and of Vatican II in general, by Pierre Lecocq, a Marxist.[18]

Lecocq distinguishes between three levels or sources of knowledge which theological discourse articulates: (1) Revealed truth,
coming from on high—immutable, definitive, possessed of an inexhaustible wealth of application; (2) Tradition—the treasure and
sum of all the convictions acquired through the centuries by the
Church in her wisdom guarding the deposit of revelation;
(3) Facts or history. The writer considers that, in *Gaudium et spes*
as in Christian thought and behaviour as a whole, everything
finally comes back to a reaffirmation of the revealed propositions:
facts are scarcely more than an opportunity to reaffirm what has

---

[16] *The Ascent of Mount Carmel*, II, 8th part, chapter 20.
[17] *Essai sur la pensée hébraïque* (Paris, 1953), p. 41.
[18] Pierre Lecocq, "La structure théologique du 'Schéma XIII' ", in
La Nouvelle Critique, 178 (August–September 1966), pp. 69–96.

already been said; concrete reality is not really a source of knowledge; "history is ultimately only an indefinite variation on the same thing, which repeats itself, becoming distorted in the process" (p. 77).

We will not attempt to satisfy the Marxist critic, for how could we, without denying our very foundations, take up a position which views as utopian and "idealist" any claim that there exists a transcendent order and that everything does not come from here below, from a purely human history? We shall remain within the bounds of biblical and Christian affirmations. But the Marxist critic does force us to recognize certain dimensions of them which perhaps have been wrongly neglected.

We must start from two exegetical data: (1) The text Exodus 3. 14 concerning the revealing of God's Name, that is to say of God himself, is increasingly being seen to mean: "I will be who (what) I will be", you will know me by my works; "I will be there with you".[19] God is the living God, he reveals himself in his works, in history which will only close at the end. (2) The biblical notion of "truth" is precisely eschatological: it is realized in that which something is called to become; it lies in front, not behind.[20] God himself is not behind the world, but in front of it, calling it on; "Christianity is not explained by the past but by the future", as Mgr Hazim, the Orthodox Metropolitan of Latakia declared magnificently in the opening speech of the Uppsala Conference in August 1968. That is also why truth *is made (se fait)*[21]—an idea which is deeply characteristic of Jewish

[19] M. Buber, "Moses" and "Königtum Gottes" reproduced in *Werke*, 11 (Kösel-Verlag, 1964); G. von Rad, *Théologie de l'Ancien Testament* (this French translation published in Geneva, 1963), p. 160; R. Reisel, *Observations on 'Ehyeh ašer 'ehyeh* (Assen, 1957); M. Allard in *Rech. Sc. Relig.*, 45 (1957), pp. 79–86; Y. Congar in *La Maison-Dieu*, 59 (1959), pp. 132–61 (reproduced in *Les voies du Dieu vivant* [Paris, 1962], pp. 80–107); R. Abba in *Journal of Biblical Literature*, 80 (1961), pp. 320–8; J. Schreiner in *Concilium* (December 1966), pp. 16–21 (American edn., vol. 20); J. B. Metz, *Gott vor uns. Ernst Bloch zu Ehren* (Frankfurt, 1965), pp. 227–41.

[20] The best account of this is given by W. Kasper, *Dogma unter dem Wort Gottes* (Mainz, 1965). Ernst Bloch is correct when he writes: "The real genesis is not situated at the beginning but at the end." (*Das Prinzip Hoffnung*, III [Berlin, 1956], p. 419.)

[21] John 3. 21; 1 John 1. 6; Tobias 4. 6; 13. 6; Ezechiel 18. 9; 2 Chronicles 31. 20. An article of mine entitled "Vie de l'Eglise et conscience de la

and Old Testament thought. The fact of Jesus Christ has altered the terms of these data without abolishing them. As Oscar Cullmann has shown, Christ anticipated the end in that moment which St Paul calls "the fullness of time", but he anticipated it by introducing into the centre or core of human history *the principle* (without the fullness of its effects) of the eschatological consummation: a new *and eternal* alliance. In one sense, then, everything is settled. There can be nothing more to add to the advent of God in person to our human nature and our world, no words to add to the Word.[22]

In an equally real sense, however, Christ's truth is still to be realized (cf. Ephesians 1. 23; 4. 15–16; Colossians 1. 19). In himself Christ is fullness, but he has to find his fullness in us. There is a non-expressed, "not yet said" side to Christ and to the Word itself which, in order to find expression, requires the variety of history and of peoples which has not yet come about. Christ is not only Alpha but Omega as well (Apocalypse 1. 8; 21. 6; 22. 13). It has been said that "man is his own future".[23] There is a future belonging to Christ, in his Body, which St Augustine called the *Christus totus, Christus integer*. There is a Christ who is to go on coming right up to his full eschatological truth: Tennyson's "the Christ that is to be".[24] What in concrete terms does this mean?

Firstly, a disclosing of Christ, and through him of God, in the

---

catholicité", in *Bulletin des Missions* (September 1938), ended with the words: "The real content of the original formula and of the texts enters the consciousness of the Church through facts: we will know what it means for the Gospel to be preached to every creature when in fact it is." This article is reprinted in *Esquisses du mystère de l'Eglise*.

[22] See chapter III of our *Jalons pour une théologie du laïcat* (Paris, 1953): references. A passage in St Thomas strikes me as appropriate: Ia IIae, q. 103, a. 3; *Lumen gentium*, art. 48: "the renovation of the world has been irrevocably decreed ... is already anticipated ...".

[23] A phrase used by Francis Pouge summarizing Heidegger's *Sein und Zeit*. Quoted by R. Garaudy, *Perspectives de l'homme* (Paris, 1960), p. 53.

[24] End of poem CV on the New Year in *In memoriam* (Everyman Library. *Tennyson's Poems* I [1830–1856], p. 331). Doubtless J. Moltmann and W. Pannenberg could be reconciled here, that is to say, the idea of the former that God will reveal himself fully at the end through the fulfilment of his promise, and the idea of the latter that history reveals God: because, for Pannenberg, only *accomplished* history reveals its total meaning and the whole of the power (royalty) of God.

lives of his saints: "the lives of the saints are also a word of God".[25] The *sensus fidelium* does not possess unqualified force but it holds an important place in theology: on occasion it becomes relevant to liturgical creations and in this way becomes involved in the production of a *lex orandi*. However, the sacramental liturgy is the archetypal context for reproducing the identical, since it is the memorial making-present of the *ephapax* of the redemption. But the Church is not simply liturgy but prophecy as well, especially in the understanding and the word which she, spurred on and sometimes summoned by history, derives from revelation and from the fact of Jesus Christ. The making-present of the Word is dependent upon other conditions than that of the redeeming actions in the sacraments. Not only is the Word of God (*gesta et dicta*) in itself possessed of infinite depth, it is above all offered to men at many different times and in many different places, experiences, problems and civilizations. Human history, with its perpetual newness and undisclosed future, on the one hand ceaselessly demands a response to questions still unknown and, on the other hand, brings with it means of expression which had not been invented previously. History, in the sense of that which confronts what has not yet come to pass, becomes in this way part of the building up of that "future of Christ" which is the life of the people of God. The people of God receives from it "the very conditions of its witness" and "the means to give its message its relevance in God's present" (Chenu). This, if we get past the rather timid terminology used, is the meaning of article 44 in *Gaudium et spes* (compare art. 58, §2) and of the idea of "signs of the times".

Concerning the problems of time and of diverse civilizations, there can be no question of simply *deducing* conclusions from the data as if they were already contained in them, pre-formed. There is no simple repetition of the same thing: the process of making present assumes and incorporates what is new and previously undisclosed. Time always goes on further. But the Holy Spirit has been given to the people of God in order to take from Christ and to carry him forward into the undisclosed historical future. He

[25] Said by Pius XI in a reference to Thérèse of Lisieux (A. Combes, *Sainte Thérèse de Lisieux et sa mission* [Paris, 1954], p. 212, n. 4).

still speaks through the prophets. As Hans Urs von Balthasar has said, he is "the unknown beyond the Word".[26] If biblical truth is at the end, he is "the Spirit of truth". A whole theology of the Holy Spirit needs to be put forward here, but that would need too much space. It is, at any rate, understandable why Jesus was able to say: "He who believes in me will do greater works than I" (John 14. 12).

The problem could be widened to include the question of whether the value of history as a branch of theology could be extended to embrace so-called profane history, the history of those outside the circle of the baptized, and, if so, under what conditions. This would take us back to the question raised at the start of this article: what meaning should be given to the word "Church"? The least that one must admit is that authentically Christian concerns or values have, historically, found their chance to develop—ambiguously but really nevertheless—outside Christian circles, sometimes in opposition to the historical Church. The Declaration of the Council, *Dignitatis humanae*, refers to this fact (art. 12, §2); Paul VI has recognized that, in one sense, the French Revolution "did nothing other than take over certain Christian ideas: fraternity, liberty, equality, progress, the desire to raise the standards of the poorer classes".[27] Can one say more than this? *Gaudium et spes* recognizes that the Holy Spirit is at work in the history of the world.[28] There exists at the moment a current of theological thought basing itself on the fact of God's union with human nature in Christ, on the existential condition in which all men find themselves owing to the fact that God's universal will for salvation has its truth in what is sometimes called objective redemption. From this, certain theologians conclude that the Church cannot be identified with the society which bears that name. The Church exists incognito in the world and in its history which are, as such, assumed into the absolute and gratuitous presence of the mystery of God: in other words, we

---

[26] "Der Unbekannte jenseits des Wortes", in *Interpretation der Welt* (Festschr. R. Guardini) (Würzburg, 1965), pp. 638–45.

[27] Sermon given on 1 September 1963 in Frascati cathedral: reported in *Osservatore Romano*, 2/3 September 1963. An extract of two-thirds of the sermon can be found in English in *The Pope Speaks*, Vol. 9, No. 2.

[28] Cf. arts. 22, §5; 26, §4; 38; 41, §1. Compare 57, §4 (the Word).

are dealing here with the notion of anonymous or implicit Christians.[29]

We cannot here undertake to discuss such a point of view. As far as the "branch of theology" aspect is concerned, formal or constituent principles which have the force of criteria ought to be brought in here: Word of God, magisterium. We come back, then, to the general rules governing theological criteriology: they apply equally to the branch known as "history". But this "branch" has an original validity and justification for itself which we have tried to outline above.

[29] The works of K. Rahner, E. Schillebeeckx and G. Baum (*supra*, n. 3) should be cited here.

Translated by Jonathan Cavanagh

Roger Aubert

Church History as an Indispensable Key to Interpreting the Decisions of the Magisterium

THE theologian's task stems from the Word of God, but this, in the Catholic perspective, is presented and applied to new situations by the Church's magisterium. One of the theologian's basic pieces of equipment, therefore, is as exact a knowledge as possible of what the magisterium has said on any particular point and the degree of authority attaching to this statement. Is a particular definition by the magisterium covered by the charism of infallibility which it enjoys in certain well-defined cases—very rare ones at that? And, if it is, what exactly has it said, what is the real point of the definition covered by the guarantee of infallibility and so to be taken as irreformable?

This inevitably involves asking oneself what question—usually very different from the ones we ask nowadays—was the magisterium tackling infallibly, what occasioned the law that still has to remain in force? If, on the other hand, we are dealing with the non-infallible magisterium, the main question—besides this one, which of course still applies—is how far its decisions continue to bind the Church and the theologian of today.

Questions of this sort inevitably arise as soon as one realizes—and it requires no great learning to do so—that Vatican II did not say exactly the same things as Vatican I on the subject of the respective places of the Pope and the bishops in the Church, or that John XXIII's views on socialism were a little different from those of Pius IX, not to speak of the not exactly negligible differences between the teaching of Boniface VIII in the Bull *Unam Sanctam* and that of Pius XII on the relationship between Church and State. If sociologists and psychologists, not to mention theologians, have something to teach us in this connection, then clearly historians also have an important part to play in answering these and related questions. This article is no more than an attempt to put forward a few thoughts along these lines, and to sketch out the direction in which it seems the answer should be sought.

I

One preliminary observation needs to be made. When we talk about theological contributions to the hermeneutic of the declarations of the magisterium, we think first of all—and this is certainly the most important part—of the history of the councils and of papal statements. But it is important not to lose sight of the fact that the decisions of the magisterium—popes, councils, bishops speaking for themselves—can only be properly understood when situated in the totality of the history of the Church. As a concrete case, take the condemnation of Jansenius in the Bull *Cum occasione* of May 1653. The case is a very pertinent one since on the one hand our understanding of the psychological context of the condemnation has been renewed by the remarkable works of Jean Orcibal and the Abbé Cognet,[1] and on the other, there are few pontifical utterances about which we know so much of the background, thanks to the researches that Lucien Ceyssens has been carrying out for the past quarter century in all the public and private archives of Western and Southern Europe. He has produced eight large volumes and more than a hundred deeply researched monographs on the subject.[2] Thanks to these works, the condemnation of the five propositions, too long approached by

[1] J. Orcibal, *Jean Duvergier de Hauranne, abbé de Saint-Cyran, et son temps* (Louvain-Paris, 1947), and *La Spiritualité de Saint-Cyran* (Paris, 1962); résumé in *Saint-Cyran et le Jansénisme*, Maîtres Spirituelles, 25 (Paris, 1961), and in *Port-Royal entre le miracle et l'obéissance* (Bruges-Paris, 1957). L. Cognet, *Le Jansénisme*, coll. "Que sais-je?", 960 (Paris, 1964), and *La Spiritualité moderne, Vol. I, L'Essor 1500–1650* (Paris, 1966), Ch. XII, "Le premier Port-Royal".
[2] These are listed up to 1963 at the head of *Miscellanea jansenistica offerts a L. Ceyssens* (Heverlee-Louvain, 1963), pp. 7–57. Cf. in particular the long introductions to *Sources relatives aux débuts du jansénisme et de l'antijansénisme, 1640–3*, Bib. de la Rev. d'Hist. Ecc., 31 (Louvain, 1957), and to *La première bulle contre Jansénius: Sources relatives à son histoire, 1644–53*, Bib. de l'Institut hist. belge de Rome, X (Brussels-Rome, 2 vols.,

theologians as the last word—which some have gone so far as to consider infallible—in a subtle discussion among specialists on the theology of grace, now appears in a very different light, and one very helpful to our present purpose.

From the end of the sixteenth century, the whole of Western Europe shows a general desire to foster a Catholic revival which would be the means of overcoming the ill effects on the Church of the double crisis of the Renaissance and the Reformation. But if the aim is held in common, the means of putting it into effect are the subject of deep divisions. Some, the Jesuits in particular, look to Christian humanism, hoping in this way to give confidence to the generations bowing down to Renaissance ideals. The spirituality they champion is often demanding, but activist in character, confident in the possibilities of man regenerated by grace. Facing this camp is another group who adopt St Augustine's more pessimistic view of man, and fear that concessions to humanism will lead to naturalism, their fear increased as they see that the pull of Calvinism on many exemplary Christians stems precisely from the desire to react against a badly Christianized humanism and so to affirm the omnipotence of grace in the work of salvation. So they come to champion a more theocentric spirituality, underlining the formidable nature of divine transcendence and sinful man's relative insignificance.

This two-pronged spiritual and pastoral option has important consequences in dogmatic and moral theology. The Christian optimism of the first group leads to Molinism and Probabilism, that is to a concept of grace as God's collaboration in effective human action and to a more indulgent view of morality. The austere and pessimistic Augustinianism of the second group led them to place a contrary stress on the role of grace in relation to human freedom and to demand a far more austere moral code. The two currents were bound to come into conflict, each being convinced that its solution was the only hope for the future of Catholicism. Gradually, under the influence of various contingent factors, it became an open quarrel, and the Jansenist dispute was originally just a new episode in this quarrel.

1961-2); also the four collections of *Jansenistica* (Malines, 1950, 1953, 1957 and 1962), and the ten collections of *Jansenistica minora* (Malines, 1950-8).

History can throw valuable light on another aspect of this episode: from beginning to end it unfolded in particularly unfortunate circumstances. These were such that disciples, or so-called disciples, of Jansenius (in fact no more than Augustinians convinced they were defending the ancient tradition of the Church against innovators whom they suspected of sacrificing too much to the tastes of the times) were ineluctably led to ask themselves, with the best will in the world, whether they were not being made victims of wicked machinations on the part of adversaries intent on covering up the weak points in their own armoury—in casuistry, for example. The fact that the condemnation was, as Ceyssens has so ably demonstrated, carried out in a singularly maladroit manner only lent fuel to their argument. This was primarily the fault of the Holy Office's Assessor, Albizzi, who played the deciding role in the see-saw events that ended in the condemnation of 1635. If theologians had been better versed in the real state of affairs in Rome at that time, they could never have dreamt of regarding the Bull *Cum occasione* as an infallible pronouncement.

Nor is this all. The declarations of the magisterium, we have seen, can only take on their true meaning in the totality of the history of the Church, which forms their context—both general and particular, as the example we have just taken shows. But the history of the Church itself only takes on value when it strives to be an overall history, resetting religious history within cultural history, against the background of the political and social, not to mention economic, history of the time. The history of Jansenism is illuminating on this point too, particularly when one takes the valid points in Lucien Goldmann's interpretation,[3] without its exaggerations and over-systematization. But there is no space here to consider this case further, and I would rather pass on to another example, that of Vatican I's definition of papal infallibility.

The Fathers who voted for the new dogma were of course

[3] Cf. *Le Dieu caché* (Paris, 1955), esp. ch. VI, "Jansénisme et noblesse de robe", and above all the intro. to *Correspondance de Martin de Barcos avec les abbesses de Port-Royal* (Paris, 1956); also the summary by R. Mandrou in *Annales: Sociétés, économie, civilization*, XII (1957), pp. 305–313.

convinced that there was nothing in valid theology to prevent this thesis being presented as binding on the faith of all believers. But why did the leaders of the majority throw themselves with such astonishing vigour into the struggle to force this definition through in the face of every obstacle? Several forceful objections were made to it on the grounds of theory and above all of opportuneness.

The reason is to be sought in the fact that its protagonists were spurred on by motives other than theological. These stemmed from the situation of the Church at the time, but also from the political and social climate of the age. Many of the Fathers in fact felt the need not only to close ranks round the supreme head of the Church against the mounting attacks of the adversaries of Rome or of Christendom, rejecting any objection to the increasing centralization of the offensive and defensive strategy of the Church; but also to underline the principle of authority as heavily as possible in a world undermined by the aspirations of democracy, which in their eyes was nothing but an attenuated form of revolutionary anarchy. Deeply influenced in their youth by traditionalism, they felt it important, for the good of society as a whole as well as for that of the Church, to emphasize hierarchical order, which quite naturally appeared to them in monarchical guise. Congar, in a penetrating article on "The Ecclesiology of the French Revolution at the Vatican Council, seen in the Affirmation of Authority",[4] has very shrewdly analysed this mentality, from which the history of the Church, and especially that of the First Vatican Council, is far from free.

Pointing out these extra-doctrinal motivations, these outside influences of a pastoral and even political character on a dogmatic decision, is not only a contribution to the detailed history of the Council, but is of real theological interest as the very form of the definition can partly be explained by the frame of mind in which its promoters approached the question. Hence that rigid, abrupt formulation that poses so many problems for theologians in the ecumenical dialogue today, with its way of presenting the infallibility and primacy of the Pope in a monarchical rather than a collegial setting. So in considering the actual definition of the

[4] In *L'Ecclésiologie au XIXe s.*, Unam Sanctam, 34 (Paris, 1960), pp. 77–114.

privileges of the Pope as it emerged in *Pastor aeternus*, it is important to take the psychological climate that produced it into account, and to distinguish the kernel of doctrine that is binding on the faithful from its superficial accretions.

II

Correct interpretation of the decisions of the ecclesiastical magisterium, then, requires them to be situated in the more general context of the secular history of the time. It follows from this that the history of each intervention must also be studied in itself, in its drafts and final forms, its long-term and short-term preparations, the pressures put on authority from one side or another, the exact circumstances in which authority finally made up its mind to speak. The magisterium of the Church is not an abstract entity, let alone a mouthpiece for the divinity, but a collection of men to whom God has confided his message for humanity with the respect due (and shown in the Incarnation) to all the laws of human psychology.

It may seem banal, but one must nevertheless insist that the historian's essential contribution to the hermeneutic of the decisions of the magisterium is simply constantly to recall their "historicity". If, as Gustav Thils has recently written, it is the case that the "reality of the Church never exists in a pure state, but is always situated at one point in history",[5] then this applies to all aspects of the Church's life, including the doctrinal definitions made by its hierarchy. These are made by men, and these men are not miraculously released from their human condition. Definitions are always made in a well-defined historical situation, in a context that inevitably colours them with the contingent factors that sound methodology requires us to take into account if we are to interpret them correctly.

There is no need to dwell on the first point, for definitions made by men are necessarily influenced by personal preoccupations, and by pressure groups—these exist in the Church as well as in the State.

The second point, though, requires more detailed consideration. Here we are at the heart of the problem, beyond those

[5] I.. *Nouv. rev. théol.*, XCI (1969), p. 484.

aspects that philosophers might dismiss as "anecdotal", however important they might be. The declarations of the magisterium, even those special cases involving a solemn dogmatic definition, are nearly always fortuitously engendered. That is to say they are occasioned by a particular historical situation to which the Church has to respond by adopting a particular position. They are also partial, in the sense that they tackle only one side of the question, and so risk concentrating attention on one controversial aspect to such an extent that, if one is not careful, this can seem to become the whole object or at least the main element in the matter under consideration.

Most of the magisterium's decisions—the whole history of the Church witnesses to this fact—have sprung from a desire to take up a position on a particular topic (which might turn out to be of marginal importance) that was under discussion in the Church at the time, or at least had come to take on particular prominence at specific moments (such as the Marian definitions, for example). Then it seemed proper to make a statement that would reaffirm a truth in danger of neglect. This is very important if the real weight and true sense of a particular definition are to be appreciated. Only too often rash speculations about a magisterial statement that has not been situated in the dogmatic whole that shows the unique mystery of Christ in its totality have led theology into blind alleys. And only too often, also, there have been attempts to discourage further reason by invoking a particular magisterial decision, whose intention was certainly not (it hardly ever is) to say the last word on the subject, but simply to clarify or even just remind people of one aspect of the question.

But this is not all, and it is not even the most essential part of the matter. Not only are the declarations of the magisterium fortuitous (produced by a contingent incident) and partial (made from a certain point of view, concerning one aspect that claimed attention at a certain moment), but they are also made within a determined cultural context. One cannot see how it could be otherwise, given that the human mind and human language are what they are, even accepting that the deliberations and even the formulations are guided by the Spirit of God: *gratia non tollit naturam*, as the old theological adage puts it with no hint of modernism. The formulas used by the magisterium, and, going

beyond the mere words, the very ideas it introduces, are conditioned by the historical intellectual situation in which every
churchman is engaged, and from which he cannot disengage himself, however hard he might try. By "historical intellectual situation" I mean simply the general mental climate of the age, the
thought processes of the age, which vary from age to age—not
radically, it is true, but measurably none the less. This means, for
our present purposes, recognizing that the theological mentality
or problematic of the age evolves as well.

Quarter of a century ago the French theologian Henri Bouillard
caused an acute scandal in certain quarters by writing: "Any
theology that is not of its age would be a false theology."[6] But this
apparently shocking statement was only the conclusion to another, less disconcerting, sentence: "When the mind evolves, an
unchanging truth can only stay the same by means of a simultaneous and correlating evolution of all its aspects, preserving the
same relationship among themselves." To say that Christian truth
can never exist in the pure state is not to say that it comes to us
with a fatal admixture of error, but just that it is always encapsul-
ated in contingent ideas and ideologies that determine its rational
structure. It is not possible to isolate it from them, since it cannot
free itself from one set of ideas except by embracing another. This
is the law of the Incarnation. Man's mind can never approach
divine truth without contingent ideas. Contingent: relative to a
particular thought system, which does not mean that the quest
for an absolute is to be abandoned, because there can be such a
thing as an absolute of affirmation, or at least of objective, over
and above the varieties of representation. If ideas, methods and
systems inevitably change with the times, the affirmations they
contain remain, but expressed in new categories. One can go
further—and follow Bouillard's meaning on from his provocative
remark: "The affirmations themselves, if they are to keep their
meaning in the new intellectual climate, determine new ideas,
methods and systems that correspond to this climate. If it were
otherwise, the old formulas would lose their original meaning by
the fact of their continuing in existence. When the mind grasps

---

[6] *Conversion et grâce chez S. Thomas d'Aquin: Etude historique*, Theologie, I (Paris, 1944), p. 219.

a formula, in fact, it tries to relate it to the totality of its conceptions in order to understand it. It interprets it in the light of what it knows. It reconstructs it according to its personal scheme of things, and only on these conditions can it understand it. Then surely it follows that if the mind unconsciously modifies one of the ideas or schemes in a formula or correlating set of formulas, then all the others have to be modified correlatively if the affirmations are to retain their original meaning?"[7]

Can it be objected that these considerations hold good for theology but not for the definitions of the magisterium? I do not think so: the magisterium can hardly define a doctrine without basing itself on theological research and without expressing itself in the thought patterns of contemporary theology.[8] So to understand exactly what it is trying to say, one has to begin with a study of what the theologians of the day were thinking, what their method of approach was, and what their thought patterns were—and this is a task for the historian.

It should not be forgotten, furthermore, that much of the definition will not only be the fruit of long-term preparatory work by theologians, but will be expressed largely in their own words, and they cannot free themselves from their own way of approaching problems and solving them. There is no need to dig in the distant past for examples: the way the documents of Vatican II were worked out is still fresh in everyone's mind. Trying to interpret encyclicals or conciliar texts without asking the historians what was in the minds of the theologians who originated them (and what their aims were) is risking a fall into grievous error, as history—again—shows happening only too often for lack of sufficient historical sensitivity.

This need to take account of the historical context of magisterial pronouncements, of the historical contingencies that give them their meaning by defining and clarifying their import, is even more pressing when one is dealing not with dogmatic statements, but with documents on moral questions, decisions that

[7] *Ibid.* Bouillard has taken the evolution of the Catholic doctrine of grace from the 12th to the 17th centuries as an illustration of this general thesis; cf. pp. 211–23.

[8] On the dependence of the magisterium on theology, in certain aspects, see Paul VI in his address to the Theological Congress in Rome: Latin and Italian texts in *L'Osservatore Romano*, 2 Oct. 1966.

concern practical behaviour. Because if dogma does not basically change but can simply be expressed differently and given greater precision, while the same applies to the basic principles of Christian morality, the applications of moral principles (or at least many of them) are subject to fluctuations brought about by changed circumstances of life and the development of understanding of the celebrated "signs of the times", which in such questions play a part whose importance has recently been stressed in the Constitution *Gaudium et Spes*.[9]

Ecclesiastical statements on moral questions, which usually come within the realm of what Mgr Montini called the "pastoral magisterium",[10] can be on different levels which it is important not to confuse. There are statements that aim to give expression to universal values on the one hand, and on the other what de Soras suggests should be called "historico-prudential assertions".[11] These would be religious appreciations of contemporary realities or ideologies in the light of universal values, and particular directives aiming at assuring that unchangeable values are expressed in changing circumstances. So, from the logical point of view, these historico-prudential assertions of the pastoral magisterium have a certain hybrid character: one viewpoint would show them as absolute and categorical assertions by virtue of the values they witness to; another would see them as assertions marked by the contingency of the historical circumstances they invoke.

They inevitably refer to gradually evolving situations or events (modern war, for example, is not exactly the same thing as war in days gone by), to institutions that evolve like all other historical phenomena (the modern business corporation, for example, is not quite the same thing as the Liberal firm of the nineteenth century), and to ideologies that are in constant process of change even if they keep the same label (mid-twentieth-century socialism compared to that of the mid-nineteenth century, for example). Here is the key to a phenomenon that so often worries people

[9] An important example will be found in the remarks by E. Schillebeeckx, "The Magisterium and the World of Politics", in *Concilium* (June 1968), pp. 12–22 (American edn. vol. 36).

[10] Article in *L'Osservatore Romano*, 13–14 May 1957.

[11] *Documents d'Eglise et options politiques* (Paris, 1962), Part II, "Comment lire et citer les documents pontificaux", esp. p. 106.

with little historical understanding: the great difference observable between one papal statement and another on the same subject. The yawning gap between the *Syllabus* of Pius IX with its condemnation of modern liberties, and the warm appreciations of the rights of man made by Pius XI and Pius XII at a time when these rights were trodden under by totalitarian regimes, is but one example among many that could be adduced if space permitted.

III

Despite the somewhat summary nature of these remarks, they do, I think, point to a definite conclusion: whether one likes it or not, the pronouncements of the magisterium are always *dated*. From this it follows that however much respect they command, one cannot reasonably accord them more than an acceptance conditioned above all by knowledge of the time and place in which they were made: in other words by their historical context. This obviously holds good for all declarations of the pastoral magisterium concerning practical conduct; it is also true to a certain extent of doctrinal definitions.

The objection could be made to this conclusion that to emphasize the historical conditioning of magisterial pronouncements is to risk voiding them of any real meaning. I do not think this is the case; in fact I am sure the opposite is true. Because it is only through recognizing the relativity of what is in fact relative that one can clearly distinguish what can justly claim to be of absolute value. It is by separating what retains a permanent validity from its historical conditioning that one protects just the permanent kernel that would otherwise be in danger of being rejected out of hand, along with what is contingent, by those intelligent enough—and their number is growing—to see what is merely contingent in all pronouncements made by men, who can never be other than men of their age.

Translated by Paul Burns

PART II
BULLETIN

Historians of the Theological Faculty
of Nijmegen University

Church History: A Survey
of Major Modern Publications

MORE than sixteen centuries ago a Palestinian bishop started the
first history of the Church with the complaint that "to undertake
such an enterprise for the first time is beyond me".[1] Subsequent
ages have shown the truth of Luke's words "that many others
have undertaken to draw up accounts of the events that have
taken place".[2] In every age people have tried to compose a survey,
compendium or synthesis of what has happened in and through
the Church.[3]

Here we offer a summary report on recent work for the guidance of the non-professional reader. This necessitated a high
degree of selectivity. We have only chosen manuals or series of a
responsible, scientific nature; general histories with an international reputation; works consisting of several volumes by various
authors; and finally, only current publications.

We finally selected for mention:

(a) A. Fliche and V. Martin (ed.), *Histoire de l'Eglise depuis
les origines jusqu'à nos jours;*[4]

[1] Eusebius of Caesarea, *Hist. Ecc.*, I, 1, 3.
[2] Luke 1. 1.
[3] An extensive survey can be found in P. Meinhold, *Geschichte der
kirchlichen Historiographie*, I–II (Orbis Academicus III, 5, Freiburg/
Munich, 1967), and a more concise one in H. Jedin, *Handbuch der Kirchengeschichte*, I (Freiburg i. Br., 1962), pp. 17–55 (English translation,
Handbook of Church History, I, pp. 1–56).
[4] Paris, 1935; of the 26 sections, 20 have appeared in 22 volumes (only
the first part has appeared of ss. 12 and 18). From 1945, the project was
directed by Fliche and E. Jarry, and after Fliche's death in 1951 by Jarry

(b) J. Jedin (ed.), *Handbuch der Kirchengeschichte*;[5] English translation, *Handbook of Church History*;

(c) L. J. Rogier, R. Aubert and M. D. Knowles (ed.), *The Christian Centuries*;[6]

(d) O. Chadwick (ed.), *The Pelican History of the Church*;[7]

(e) K. D. Schmidt and E. Wolf (ed.), *Die Kirche in ihrer Geschichte. Ein Handbuch.*[8]

We shall start with a very brief and general description of these five publications, and then offer some detailed observations, period by period, in order to help the theologically interested reader to make his own choice.[9]

I. GENERAL DESCRIPTION

(a) At present the most extensive and also the oldest of the five publications is the one started by the well-known medievalist of Montpellier, Augustin Fliche, who died in 1951. This great enterprise, clearly marked by the "Catholic renewal" of the kind that prevailed between the two world wars, was launched in 1935 under the direction of Fliche and Victor Martin, who died in 1945 and did not himself contribute to it as a writer. The plan and its execution are not exactly models of editorial teamwork. The value of the various parts is very uneven and very dependent

---

and J. B. Duroselle. In the Italian translation, under Pietro Frutaz (Turin, 1938 f.), footnotes and references have been brought up to date.

[5] Freiburg i. Br., 1962; of the six volumes three have appeared (vol. III in two parts); in English, vols. I and III are available.

[6] The work is published in Dutch, French, German, Spanish, Portuguese, Italian and English. The English edition (London and New York) will have five volumes of which two have appeared. Of the Italian edition nothing has appeared as yet.

[7] Penguin Books, 1960; 6 volumes are planned, 5 have appeared.

[8] Göttingen, 1961, planned in four parts, distributed over about 40 instalments, of which 11 have appeared so far.

[9] Lack of space has limited us to a mention of only a few of the many aspects. For the same reason we have had to cut out mention of reviews, but most volumes have been discussed in RHE. For general considerations and critical problems, see, *int. al.*, E. Benz, *Kirchengeschichte in ökumenisher Sicht* (Ökumenische Studien, 3, Leiden/Cologne, 1961), and various articles in *L'histoire et l'historien* (Rech. et débats du Centre cath. des intellectuels français, 47, Paris, 1964), e.g., R. Aubert, *loc. cit.*, pp. 28-43; D. Julian, *loc. cit.*, pp. 87-94; J. Bouveresse, *loc. cit.*, pp. 166-77.

on the competence of each of the forty collaborators. In general, it is dominated by the "political", "external" aspect of Church history, although there are some parts with excellent analyses of the "internal" one. The fact that the pre-war volumes (1 to 8, inc.) have not been brought up to date, the absence of indexes (till 1956), and the slow pace of publication, constitute a grave deficiency.[10]

(b) Jedin's *Handbook* is in a very different situation. The German publishers, Herder, issued the first volume in 1962. They published Kirsch before the war and Hergenröther in the nineteenth century. Well prepared by an editorial team under the direction of Hubert Jedin, and with an editor-in-chief for each volume, this work has become one of the most reliable works of reference now available.

Much attention is paid to the "internal" aspect of Church history. Because of the careful selection of collaborators (fourteen in all, mainly German) planning and treatment are well unified and show a comprehensive vision. That the text and bibliography of some sections were finalized some years before publication is a pity in this otherwise able work.[11]

(c) Very different again is the history organized by Rogier, Aubert and Knowles (editors), with Anton Weiler as editorial secretary. It is published in nine countries simultaneously and is, as such, the first truly international publication of its kind.

Each of the seven authors is in charge of a specific period although three specialists have been mustered for the Eastern Churches. The advantages of such an arrangement are obvious: a better chance of unity for each period, uniformity of style and taut composition.

In spite of the splendid introduction by Aubert, the aim of the series remains somewhat vague: what kind of audience is

[10] Apart from the volumes that are still incomplete (see n. 4) the following are still to be done: vols. 11 (Avignon), 22–23 (recent history), 24 (Eastern Churches) and 25 (Protestant Churches), while vol. 26 will contain the indexes. Other series also treat the non-Catholic Churches separately and bring in specialists, but the volume covering a given period constitutes more of a whole than in the Fliche–Martin project.

[11] Cf. the preface to III/1 (1966), p. viii: "in the space of about five years", and the additional bibliography in IV (1967), pp. 684–6.

envisaged? Is it the professional historian, the theologian, the intellectual or the interested Christian? According to the publisher's prospectus it is all of them. But this broad approach has its drawbacks: too much detail for the one and too little scientific documentation for the other; it is neither a manual nor a book for simple reading, and the illustrations, however unusual, do little to correct this.[12]

(d) On this point, it is interesting to compare this publication with the Pelican History of the Church. The latter follows the same principle of one author for each volume and a practically total absence of scientific apparatus. The aim, however, seems more definite and clearer: easily readable and comprehensive sections for the layman who, though no expert, is genuinely interested.

That this series appears in paperback is typical. In general, English scholarship has achieved a *tour de force* which makes some volumes almost bedside books. If in England, proportionately speaking, Christendom is too often overstressed, the same holds, *mutatis mutandis*, for practically every handbook.[13]

(e) Very different again is the Church history published in Göttingen which explicitly aims at being a handbook. It is clearly Protestant in character and very specific in its lay-out. Forty specialists, practically all German, concentrate not so much on periods as on themes. The sections therefore appear in random sequence and almost independently of each other. The drawbacks this creates for a synthesis of Church history are obvious: it simply is not attempted. Over against this, however, we have here a professional treatment of given themes in an extremely

[12] The choice and explanation of the illustrations are the work of G. Beekelaar and G. Lemmens; the French edition has no illustrations. The fact that an international co-operative venture has not even managed to organize an international reference system is a serious defect which proves that either the level of scientific writing remains nationalistic, or that the publisher's interests prevail, or both.

[13] This holds, for instance, for Fliche and Martin, where the French character of the work has led to an almost complete ignoring of the Scandinavian countries; see also R. Aubert in his introduction to the Dutch edition of *The Christian Centuries*, where he points out that historiography of the Church so frequently and tenaciously remains confined to "the Vienna-Brussels-Cadiz-Naples quadrangle" (p. xxiv).

concise manner. In so far as bibliography and references are concerned, Schmidt and Wolf are without doubt outstanding among
the works here discussed.[14a]

II. The Five Works compared Period by Period

The following figures may give some insight into the arrangement of the material, and the editors' interests, and so be a
starting-point for the more detailed comparison of the five publications.[14b] We have divided the whole history into four periods:
the early Church (A.D. 1–700), the Middle Ages (700–1500), the
period after the Middle Ages up to the French Revolution (1500–
1789) and modern times (1789–1970).

	Fliche	Jedin	Rogier	Pelican	Schmidt	Total Average
A.D. 1–700:	17%	28%	21%	16%	16% —	20%
700–1500:	40%	29%	19%	14%	20% —	24%
1500–1789:	25%	25%	29%	30%	28% —	27%
1789–1970:	18%	18%	31%	40%	36% —	29%
	100	100	100	100	100	100

1. *The Early Church* (A.D. 1–700)

(*a*) In the first four volumes of Fliche-Martin, the first three
centuries are dealt with by J. Lebreton and J. Zeiller; the period
from the peace of Constantine to the death of Theodosius, by
J. R. Palanque, G. Bardy and P. de Labriolle; and the fifth and
sixth centuries (till 590) by Bardy, de Labriolle, L. Bréhier and
G. de Plinval.[15]

[14a] The footnotes frequently occupy more space on a page than the text.
Unfortunately, some volumes show carelessness in quotations and references.

[14b] Since none of the five publications is complete, the percentages are
clearly approximate; for the missing volumes the proportions were esti-
mated on the basis of the published material and the prospectuses. For
volume VI of the Pelican History we have taken the state of the distribution of the four periods as the basis of our estimate.

[15] J. Lebreton and J. Zeiller, *L'Eglise primitive* (Fl.-M., I, Paris, 1934);
De la fin du 2e siècle à la paix constantinienne (Fl.-M., II, Paris, 1935).
These two volumes have been translated by E. C. Messenger under the
title: *The History of the Primitive Church* (London, 1942–8, and New
York, 1949), and have been republished (New York, 1962) under the

These parts were written with the help of the rediscovery of patristics and were published between 1934 and 1937. They are not only well documented but are still the most complete history of the early Church as a whole.

Since then new fields of study have been opened up, such as Judaeo-Christianity and the gnosis, and this has made the historiography of the first and second centuries (here still called the "primitive" Church) a matter of much more careful qualification. Moreover, during the last thirty years a number of scholarly monographs have produced much new material—one has but to think of the history of the councils.

The volumes here discussed consist in fact of a number of monographs, planned and worked out independently. In spite of the intentions of the editors, little attention has been paid to the social aspect of the Church and to the diversity of the various groups of Christians. On the other hand, one can hardly expect a previous generation to satisfy all the wishes of the present one.

(b) In Jedin's *Handbook*, Karl Baus wrote the whole of the first part, which deals with the period from the original community to the early Christian Church as a whole (*Grosskirche*),[16] that is, up to the "conversion" of Constantine. The Greek and Latin history of the Church of the second half of the second century and the whole of the third is particularly well written and is based directly on first-hand sources.

The author has particularly concentrated on Christian ideas, so that the various schools of theology and their authors stand out clearly.

(c) In the Rogier, Aubert and Knowles history, the first three centuries are tackled by Jean Daniélou, while Henri Marrou has dealt with the period from Diocletian to the death of Gregory the Great.[17] Daniélou's contribution is unsatisfactory: the treatment

---

(better!) title: *A History of the Early Church*. J. R. Palanque, G. Bardy and P. de Labriolle, *De la paix constantinienne à la mort de Théodose* (Fl.-M., III, Paris, 1936); P. de Labriolle, G. Bardy, L. Bréhier, G. de Plinval, *De la mort de Théodose à l'élection de Grégoire le Grand* (Fl.-M., IV, Paris, 1937); these two volumes have also been translated by Messenger under the title: *The Church in the Christian Empire* (London/New York, 1949).

[16] *Loc. cit.*, first edn. 1962, 3rd edn. 1965.

[17] J. Daniélou, "The Origins to the End of the Third Century", in

is not rounded off, the phenomenon of Judaeo-Christianity has been over-emphasized and the detailed treatment is sometimes confusing.

Marrou's text, on the other hand, is much better organized and more instructive. It is written in essay style and such chapters as those dealing with Nicaea and Arianism are, for all their brevity, little masterpieces of comprehensive clarity. Marrou takes the development of the later Roman Empire as a constant factor for the period from Diocletian to the fall of Constantinople in 1453. But in the fifth century and afterwards one observes a latent break between the Eastern and the Western world, and so he treats the two Churches separately from that time on.

(d) In the first part of Owen Chadwick's Pelican History, Henry Chadwick has given us a smooth and masterly introduction.[18] He gives full treatment to the "internal" development of Christian society. He, too, is aware of the growing tension between East and West since the fourth century. He has dealt with the period from the beginning till Gregory the Great inclusive.

(d) Of Schmidt and Wolf's handbook, so far only one instalment has appeared and this deals with early Christianity. Leonhard Goppelt here deals with the apostolic and post-apostolic age. He sees the latter as the transition period from the apostolic age to early Catholicism (*Frükatholizismus*), covering the years 70 to 135.[19]

At present, this is the newest and best-documented treatment of the first one and a half centuries of Christianity. Well at home in the history of Judaeo-Christianity, the author gives us a theologically penetrating and historically expert analysis in which systematic and intelligent use has been made of the most recent literature. The names of the authors in charge of the remaining instalments, among them G. Kretschmar, W. Schneemelcher and H. G. Beck, lead one to assume that this first part will become the

---

vol. I, *The First Six Hundred Years* (London, 1964), pp. 1–220, and H. Marrou, "The Great Persecution to the Emergence of Medieval Christianity", *ibid.*, pp. 223–458.

[18] H. Chadwick, *The Early Church* (Pelican History, London, 1967), vol. I.

[19] L. Goppelt, *Die apostolische und nachapostolische Zeit* (Schmidt–Wolf, I A, first edn. 1962, 2nd edn. 1966).

most important reference work for the study of Christian antiquity.

2. *The Middle Ages (700–1500)*

(*a*) Fliche and Martin have spread the Middle Ages over ten volumes and nineteen authors. Of the more than five thousand pages which appeared between 1939 and 1964 (only "Avignon" is still lacking), Fliche himself was responsible for more than one-fifth. The meaning, character and continuity of the Gregorian reform are therefore heavily stressed and interpreted according to his personal views.

The chronological treatment of the period is interrupted in volume 12 by a masterly sociological and historical analysis of medieval Christian institutions by G. Le Bras (still, unfortunately, a skeleton of what this author could give us), and in volume 13 by a clear *exposé* of medieval thought by, among others, van Steenberghen for the thirteenth century.[20]

These two contributions fill the gaps left in the other volumes in a felicitous way, and are particularly useful for the theologian. The most recent publication, two volumes on the age of conciliarism, shows most clearly the influence of the new theological insights.[21]

(*b*) Volume III of Jedin's *Handbook* was originally intended to cover the period from 700–1300. Volume IV would then take the later Middle Ages and the sixteenth century together. For reasons that are not very clear, this plan was abandoned, and now III/1 and III/2 cover the whole of the Middle Ages from 700 to 1500, distributed over eight authors, among whom F. Kempf and H. Wolter contribute the lion's share.[22] The sections written by Kempf show the results of modern studies of

---

[20] G. Le Bras, *Institutions ecclésiastiques de la Chrétienté médiévale.* Préliminaires et première partie, *loc. cit.*, 1959–64 (the complicated division into six books does not correspond to the announcement on p. 232). A. Forest, F. van Steenberghen and M. de Gandillac, *Le mouvement doctrinal du IXe au XIVe siècle*, *loc. cit.*, 1951.

[21] E. Delaruelle, R. E. Labande and P. Ourliac, *L'Eglise au temps du Grand Schisme et de la crise conciliaire, 1378–1449* (Fl.-M., XIV, 1962–64).

[22] Thus Kempf in III/I for the tenth, eleventh and the first quarter of the twelfth centuries, and Wolter in III/2 for the twelfth and thirteenth centuries (publ. resp. in 1966 and 1968).

medieval canon law; the controversial history of the medieval papacy and the "internal" history of the Church have been amended in an original way. Beck's contribution on the Byzantine Church and Jungmann's on the liturgy and popular devotion should clear up much traditional misunderstanding in matters of history.

(c) At the same time that Jedin's III/2 apeared, M. D. Knowles produced his volume on the Middle Ages in *The Christian Centuries*.[23] He is a good raconteur. In effect, he tells some forty-two short, sometimes very clever, stories in essay form, each dealing with one aspect, using data that is chronologically disparate. This causes the historical treatment to proceed in leaps and bounds, while his anecdotal way of writing resembles the style of the medieval chronicle. It is true that the "internal" aspect is done full justice in the volume as a whole. But to separate secular history from Church history, even in the chronological tables, would seem to be a somewhat arbitrary undertaking for the Middle Ages.

(d) In the Pelican History, the Middle Ages will be treated by Robert Southern.

(e) Schmidt and Wolf's *Handbook* is also incomplete as regards the Middle Ages. Of the five planned sections, only three and a half have so far been published. Grundmann's history of heresy is worth special mention. It is a concise and clear treatment of essentials.[24] Of special importance for the theologian is the last published instalment by M. A. Schmidt (not the editor-in-chief). He has managed to give in a very brief space a synthesis of scholasticism in such a clever form and so richly provided with sources, references and a truly international bibliography, that one readily forgives the inadequate treatment of the "external" history in the other instalments of this work.[25]

3. *From the End of the Middle Ages to the French Revolution*
   (1500–1789)

(a) Of the Fliche and Martin volumes which cover this period

---

[23] *The Middle Ages* (*The Christian Centuries*, vol. II, 1968).

[24] H. Grundmann, *Ketzergeschichte des Mittelalters* (Schmidt–Wolf, II G1, 1968).

[25] M. A. Schmidt, *Scholastik* (Schmidt–Wolf, II G2, 1969).

it may be said that they are mainly written without reference to post-war German and Scandinavian historiography. Thus L. Cristiani's study of the Tridentine period has been outdated by Jedin's standard work. Moreover, the post-Tridentine period, undertaken by L. Willaert (who has since died), is an untidy piece of writing.

Still important for reference purposes are the brief but penetrating analyses of the Renaissance and the beginning of the sixteenth century by Aubenas and Ricard, as well as the extensive synthesis of Church life in the second half of the seventeenth and the whole of the eighteenth centuries by Préclin and Jarry.[26] This last volume, particularly, contains material in its modern treatment of eighteenth-century Gallicanism which will interest the theologically-minded reader.

(b) The obvious choice for the treatment of the division in the Church of the sixteenth century in Jedin's Handbook was E. Iserloh, disciple and rival of Lortz, and one of the greatest living authorities on Luther. He tackles this in a very learned exposé with constant reference to the sources in volume IV. It is a pity, however, that this history of the Reformation offers so little about Calvin and Calvinism and still less about the Baptist movement.

The editor-in-chief, who has already published an excellent history of Trent and its antecedents, here relates the story of the interconnecting movements of the "Catholic Reform" and the "Counter-Reformation". For both authors, the writing of history always implies theological reflection, and in their preface they state explicitly that their approach has been "in the spirit of Catholicism and ecumenism".[27] The period dealt with here takes the reader up to 1655.

J. Glazik wrote the section on the history of the missions, also in this volume. In volume V, L. Cognet and H. Raab will deal with the seventeenth century in France, while the history of the missions will be the responsibility of P. Beckmann.

(c) Volume III of The Christian Centuries covers the sixteenth and seventeenth centuries and is entrusted to H. Tüchle. The

[26] R. Aubenas, R. Ricard, L'Eglise et la Renaissance, 1449–1517 (Fl.-M., XV, 1951). E. Préclin, E. Jarry, Les luttes politiques et doctrinales aux XVIIe et XVIIIe siècles (Fl.-M., XIX, 2 vols., 1955–56).
[27] Loc. cit., p. vi.

author has not worried overmuch about the historiographic, and the (for this period) theologically loaded, problems of the period, as is clear from the traditional terminology used in his choice of title: "Reformation and Counter-Reformation".[28] His intention is to introduce the uninitiated to the *story* of the division of the Church in the sixteenth century, and its consequences.

The volume closes with a learned contribution by C. A. Bouman about the Churches of the Byzantine rite in the Ottoman empire.

The eighteenth century (vol. IV) has been dealt with by Rogier in his own typical style and consists of a smaller number of well-set-out analytical surveys. For an internationally conceived history, though, the history of the Church in Holland occupies an over-generous amount of space.[29]

(*d*) The third volume of the Pelican History, by Owen Chadwick himself, gives a very concise and smoothly written survey of the changes which took place within Christianity during the sixteenth century and the first half of the seventeenth.

In volume IV, Gerald Cragg treats of the period from 1648 to 1789, perhaps over-concentrating on England, but with an excellent description within this narrow scope of the rise and continuing development of rationalism.[30]

(*e*) While Iserloh turned the analysis of the German Reformation into a monograph on Luther, F. Lau tried in the Schmidt and Wolf *Handbook*, perhaps rather rashly, to describe the first decades of the same story while by-passing the fate of Luther. But in doing so, he was consistent with the purpose of this history, which plans a separate treatment of the three great Reformers, Luther, Zwingli and Calvin.

The author has his own clear idea about the German Reformation: it is no doubt rooted in what he calls "the case of Luther"

[28] In the Dutch edn. the first part of the Reformation appeared in 1968, the second in 1966.

[29] In the Dutch edn. L. J. Rogier's contribution on the Church in the age of Enlightenment and Revolution, 1715–1801 (vol. VII, 1964), the Netherlands and the Netherlanders are referred to 60 times explicitly and 13 times in passing, in a total of 300 pages.

[30] O. Chadwick, *The Reformation* (Pel. Hist., III, first edn. 1964, 3rd edn. 1968); G. R. Cragg, *The Church and the Age of Reason, 1648–1789* (Pel. Hist., IV, first edn. 1960, 2nd edn. 1966).

but nevertheless develops into an irreducible multiplicity of reform movements and ecclesial structures. In other words, the
author attempts an outline of the structures of the German Reformation. He takes the story up to 1532, where E. Bizer takes
over and provides an excellent survey of the further development
until 1555.[31]

In contrast with Iserloh, who constantly leaves the word to his
spokesmen, Lau and Bizer never lead the reader beyond the
threshold of their sources. These sources are gathered, together
with numerous references, in an awe-inspiring apparatus of notes.

For the remaining centuries, we only have Heyer who provides
a sound survey of the history of the Catholic Church from 1648
till 1870.[32]

4. *Modern Times* (1789–1970)

(*a*) The Fliche–Martin history planned to cover this period in
six volumes but only two have appeared so far: Leflon has taken
the years between 1789 and 1846, Aubert the pontificate of Pius
IX.[33] As is the case with all the other works, the way the phenomenon of revolution is handled is central for this period: how to
interpret the revolutionary trends at various levels, and what are
the attitudes taken up by the Churches in this respect. It is precisely on this point that there is a vast difference between volumes
20 and 21.

On the whole, Leflon has not been very successful: his plan is
unsatisfactory (one-third of the text is devoted exclusively to the
French Revolution, two-thirds to the four pontificates of the first
half of the nineteenth century), the image of the Church is, to say
the least, debatable ("revolution" is seen as a threat to the established Church, and so the main burden of the whole is a matter
of external ecclesiastical politics), and finally, the preoccupation
with apologetics is rather too obvious. There is, however, an

---

[31] F. Lau, E. Bizer, *Reformationsgeschichte Deutschlands bis 1555*
(Schmidt–Wolf, III K, 1964).
[32] F. Heyer, *Die katholische Kirche vom Westfälischen Frieden bis zum
Ersten Vatikanischen Konzil* (Schmidt–Wolf, IV N1, 1963).
[33] J. Leflon, *La crise révolutionnaire, 1789–1846* (Fl.-M., XX, 1951);
R. Aubert, *Le pontificat de Pie IX, 1846–1878* (Fl.-M., XXI, first edn.
1952, 2nd edn. 1963).

abundance of information, and the attempt to arrive at a balanced judgment in this complex problem shows progress in Catholic historical writing on the French Revolution.

Aubert, on the other hand, manages to combine all that belongs in a handbook. He has the talent to arrange facts, trends, persons and their interconnection in an orderly narrative. Here the Church appears on the public stage, and her contact with the revolutionary society of those days is shown as arising from her own condition. In this gently critical and universal biography of the Church and her visible head one finds, with a vast quantity of fascinating material, the absorbing story of a Church that finds herself, with all her weaknesses and attractions, at a turning-point in history. Anyone who wants to understand the Church of the twentieth century cannot afford to ignore Aubert's book.

(b) In Jedin's *Handbook*, the demarcation line between volumes V and VI is drawn at 1815. Contrary to an earlier announcement, the main authors will be Aubert and R. Lill.

(c) *The Christian Centuries* is not yet complete, so no final judgment is yet possible. So far we have the contributions by Rogier (mentioned here under 3c) and Bertier de Sauvigny. The former provides a good narrative with an interesting personal view but one misses various points brought out in recent French writing, and one would have liked more about the non-Catholic Churches. De Sauvigny writes well about the Restoration period, but it is not clear why so much space should be set apart in this publication for a period (1801–48) where we look in vain for that "awakening of spiritual forces" suggested by the author.[34]

The period from 1848 to 1970 will be undertaken by five authors: Rogier and Aubert for the nineteenth and twentieth centuries, Tracy Ellis for North and South America, Hajjar and Bruls for the Eastern Churches and the missions.

(d) Volume V of the Pelican History is the work of Alec Vidler who has dealt with the period from 1789 till today in twenty-three small chapters, the choice of which looks somewhat arbitrary. Eleven of these chapters are concerned with the Anglo-Saxon Churches. As a final part of a series that aims at the general

---

[34] G. de Bertier de Sauvigny, *The Church in the Age of Restoration, 1801–1848, loc. cit.* (1965).

public, this smallest of the five volumes might have given us something more about the last decades.[35]

The series concludes with a masterly treatment of the history of the missions by S. Neill.[36] He provides a survey of the whole missionary activity displayed by the Christian Churches throughout history, but concentrates on the nineteenth and twentieth centuries. It is true that one does not always see the link between this activity and what was happening on the ecclesiastical homefront, but this drawback is outweighed by the advantage of a clear and fascinating synthesis.

(e) For the modern age, in particular, the Schmidt–Wolf *Handbook* has the advantage of a loose editorial organization: the absence of a fixed total project has worked in favour of the treatment of details. The four instalments of volume IV which have appeared so far are excellent monographs, clear in style and arrangement, and solid in content.[37]

Heyer's contribution, mentioned under 3(e), will be continued from Vatican I onwards by G. Maron. Beyreuther's small essay on the "revival movement" is important precisely from the point of view of "ecclesial" history. The recent history of the missions by Gensichen gives a fair amount of space to the Catholic missions.[38] Lastly, there is the fascinating treatment of the German *Landeskirchen* (State-Churches) in the nineteenth and twentieth centuries. Among other things, the author tries to trace the causes of the Hitler period and the attitude of the Protestant Churches at the time of Nazism. While not making use of all the new monographs, the author bases his writing on the sources and

---

[35] A. R. Vidler, *The Church in an Age of Revolution* (Pel. Hist., V, 1961).

[36] S. Neill, *A History of Christian Missions* (Pel. Hist., VI, first edn. 1964, 2nd edn. 1966).

[37] The last volumes of part III run on to the present age. K. Onasch, *Grundzüge der russischen Kirchengeschichte* (Schmidt–Wolf, III, M 1) has already appeared (1967). Of part IV the following "national" sections have been published: P. Kawerau, *Kirchengeschichte Nordamerikas*, M. Begrich, *Kirchengeschichte Brasiliens im Abriss*, and M. Jacobs, *Die Kirchengeschichte Südamerikas spanischer Zunge* (Schmidt–Wolf, IV S, 1963).

[38] Heyer, see n. 32; E. Beyreuther, *Die Erweckungsbewegung* (Schmidt–Wolf, IV R, 1963); H. W. Gensichen, *Missiongeschichte der neueren Zeit* (Schmidt–Wolf, IV T, 1961).

brings a sector of Church history to life again. One looks forward to the "Catholic" companion to this volume.[39]

The award of accolades in this context would have little meaning. Frequent use of the five publications discussed shows that advantages and disadvantages will be seen differently according to what the reader looks for in a handbook and according to the choice that guided the editors and authors. The perfect handbook will never be written. To have had the courage to attempt such great things—and who would deny that Church history is a great matter?—is a merit in itself.

ADELBERT DAVIDS
LOUIS GOOSEN
EUGÈNE HONÉE
JAN VAN LAARHOVEN

[39] K. Kupisch, *Die deutschen Landeskirchen im 19. und 20. Jahrhundert* (Schmidt-Wolf, IV R 2, 1966); G. Maron's *Die katholische Kirche seit dem Vatikanum* (Schmidt-Wolf, IV N 2) has been announced as forthcoming.

Translated by Theo Westow

Jacques Gadille

Sociology and Religious History: A General View of the Literature

IT HAS been said quite rightly that religious history has been "invaded" by sociology.[1] The latter's development is well illustrated by the international bibliography of its output compiled by H. Carrier and E. Pin (313 pages for the period 1900–61). The same authors have just published a supplement to this—a volume of almost the same length (305 pages) merely for the years 1962–1966.[2]

And yet it can hardly be said that historians are very familiar with this vast amount of work which they consider as abstract, ephemeral and too "philosophical". History and sociology need to have greater knowledge of each other and even to make their methods complementary. This was recently pointed out by G. Cholvy.[3] The divergence lies deeper than merely mutual apathy or neglect; it is to be found in the way in which problems are approached. Religious sociology to a great extent came into being between the two wars at a time of growing awareness of the increasing religious indifference of the masses; as a consequence, and of set purpose, it turned its attention more to the actual practice of the majority than to the study of the institution itself or of its more prominent members; it was more concerned with

[1] J. Glenisson in *Vingt cinq ans de recherche historique en France, 1940–1965,* C.N.R.S. (Paris, 1965), XXXIX.
[2] H. Carrier, E. Pin, *Sociologie du Christianisme. Bibliographie internationale* (Rome, 1964). The same with A. Fasola Bologna, *Supplément, 1962–1966 (ibid.,* 1968).
[3] G. Cholvy, "Sociologie religieuse et histoire", in *Revue d'histoire de l'Eglise de France",* vol. LV (January–June 1969, 6).

the religion of the people than the "religion of books". It paid particular attention to accurate census figures and the analysis of actual situations, to a recurrent sociography, and for their inter pretation to theoretical explanatory diagrams like the relation between religious practice and the size of the population centres or the professional categories at income or cultural level. Sociological interpretation rarely appealed to history. It investigated rather those centres already disturbed by economic disruption or contemporary social upheaval rather than traditional societies. Even before the war, of course, G. Le Bras and his disciple F. Boulard on their own account had drawn attention to the history of religious practice in rural societies, but in that too they were pioneers.[4] The other tendency emerges clearly from the analytical headings in the bibliographies quoted above.[5] The lead given by Le Bras was only to be found reflected in general historical works at a fairly recent date, and especially after 1960: these were the theses by J. Toussaert on the Flemish countryside at the end of the Middle Ages (1959), by J. Ferté on country districts of the Paris region in the seventeenth century (1962) and of Ch. Marcilhacy on the Orléans district in the middle of the nineteenth century (1963-4).

But it must be noticed that, unlike studies in religious sociology in the proper sense of the term, urban centres were excluded from these studies. It was not until G. Cholvy's book that for the first time the statistical rules of religious sociology were applied to a whole diocese at once. G. Le Bras in the preface called this a real treatise on the subject. Now this thesis was submitted at the University of Montpellier in October 1967. Its author acknowledged that his fundamental principle of interpretation of the diocesan Mass census on a certain Sunday in 1962 was the history of this diocese. At present he is engaged in writing about the whole period of the Concordat, thus furnishing a good example of what E. Bloch termed the regressive method.[6]

[4] "Bibliographie des écrits de G. Le Bras", in Etudes de droit canonique dediées à G. Le Bras, vol. I (Paris, 1965).

[5] Preponderance of some fifty articles on the subject of towns under the heading "parishes" (Sociologie du christianisme, 1964, pp. 261-4) and the unequal treatment given to countryside and towns.

[6] G. Cholvy, Géographie religieuse de l'Hérault contemporain (Publications de la Faculté des Lettres et Sciences de Montpellier, 32) (Paris, 1968).

A year later, taking the human groups in their complex reality and comparing town and country, F. Boulard and J. Rémy revealed "cultural regions": in them they saw the ultimate key to differences of religious practice. To bring out clearly this idea of "cultural regions" these authors appealed to history and to the family as the principal agent in the handing down of traditions.[7]

Lastly, the greater expansion under certain headings like Religious Disaffection, Religious Pluralism, History of Religious Practice, Messianic Movements, Millenarianism and Syncretism, and especially Religious and Socio-Cultural Changes,[8] are evidence of the greater attention paid to history by religious sociologists. This development was not accidental. It is a result of the inadequacy of the classical methods of sociological conditioning for the correct interpretation of the levels of religious practice and of the need for recourse to long series. The charts in religious sociology have a tendency to show disparities in homogeneous and clearly defined units. The appeal to history offers the possibility of a more accurate view of the discontinuities and the changes in religious practice from one generation to another within the framework of a same region. It gives greater sensitivity to the plasticity of this religious psycho-sociology in relation to what G. Cholvy calls the internal and external factors, but also in relation to the "event".

The bringing together of the two branches is therefore a recent acquisition; it has proved the more fruitful in that it obliges sociologists and religious historians reciprocally to correct their methods. A simple analytical list of the studies of historical religious sociology, of which there are still only a few, would have little meaning. This short survey of the applications of religious sociology to history leads rather to critical reflection; I should like this to be impartial on both heads.

At the outset an introductory remark about sources is necessary. Everyone knows that the statistical preoccupations of "social mathematics" came to the fore among philosophers, and also among certain prelates, only at the end of the eighteenth century.

---

[7] F. Boulard and J. Rémy, with the collaboration of M. Decreuse, *Pratique urbaine et régions culturelles*, Supplément, pp. 192–4 and *passim*
[8] *Sociologie du Christianisme. Supplément . . .*, pp. 192–4 and *passim*.

In the nineteenth century the first French bishops who were concerned to investigate the exact religious situation of their dioceses in the 'forties tended to belong to the "liberal Catholic" group— Rivet of Dijon, Ravinet at Troyes and Dupanloup through whom Mme Marcilhacy had access to exceptional documentary resources. All the same, investigations of this kind and reports on visitations are principally concerned with the state of the accounts, church buildings and even vestments. More so, when the earlier periods are considered: the statistics that Abbé Toussaert managed to establish had to contend with the almost total absence of demographic statistical data. Principally of course it is the religious significance of the activity investigated that must be submitted to critical examination. No sign must be left out of account and, in the case of Catholicism, the carrying out of the Sunday obligation and, more especially, Easter duties assumes a far greater importance than for other religions, as has been pointed out.[9] Very properly, M. Chaunu has emphasized that the almost universal practice of religion during the last centuries of the *ancien régime* was rather the expression of a religious conformism which at the Revolution came to be manifested differently, merely changing from practice to non-practice. The same could be said of priestly or religious vocations, at least until 1830; they might depend on considerations of status or social advancement. Thus the criteria selected had to be interpreted by the milieu in which they occurred, and more qualitative criteria had to be chosen: those which, in G. Le Bras's phrase, were an expression of "religious vitality". And so, with regard to recruitment to the priesthood particular note was made of missionary vocations, and concerning people's adherence to the Church attention was paid especially to participation in individual charitable works, what Dupanloup called "activities of zeal". All the same it will not be forgotten that L. Perouas has obtained from statistics of a more material nature (gifts to the clergy, church maintenance or building accounts) valuable information about the level of religious fervour in one or two parishes of the diocese of La Rochelle under the *ancien régime*; the quest for the qualitative criterion by no means excludes consideration of more everyday actions, even the most

[9] Travulle, "Problèmes méthodologiques d'une recherche sur la signification de la messe", in *Social Compass*, 11 (1965), pp. 37-46.

9—C.

material when they bear some relation to the institutional Church. The same author had access to an exceptionally long series of ordination registers but he was careful to compare this material with all the other sources of information available instead of studying it separately. Another source, derived from the religious practice statistics, has been discovered. This is the delays occurring in the baptism of infants made use of by Diebold in the Eure department, Bizeau for Chartres and Charpin at Marseilles.[10] But, as Cholvy has shown, increase in these delays is entirely compatible with religious fervour in those places where the canonical rules have been somewhat relaxed or merely where infant mortality has decreased. On the other hand, observance of only a short delay might well be the sign of a recurrent conformism in parts of the country that are growing increasingly indifferent to religion.

The sociologist, then, has found fresh sources of information in the dormant masses mentioned by economists and demographers, but it is the historian who shows him how to collate them and compare their fluctuations on a long-term basis. In this way M. Vovelle assessed the degree of religious fervour in Provence in the last century of the *ancien régime* from bequests in wills for the foundation of votive Masses and, more recently, on the basis of the distribution and iconography in churches and chapels of the altarpieces put up by the faithful in their devotion to the souls in purgatory. In this way, too, M. Agulhon showed the importance of the confraternities as an indication of the social and religious life of these same parts of the country.[11] On the other hand, reliance on the mere statistics of sacramental practice, particularly in a region artificially cut off from the external factors influencing it and even in the confined limits of the rural parish, carries with it some danger of giving an admittedly clear picture of the reality, but an incomplete one through neglect of the more classical materials (important works of spirituality, teaching

[10] See *Archives de sociologie des religions*, 19 (1965), pp. 180–3, note 122, on the subject; F. L. Charpin, *Pratique religieuse et formation d'une grande ville* (Paris, 1962), and F. Boulard, *Premières itinéraires*, pp. 122, 123.

[11] G. Vovelle, *Vision de la mort et de l'au-delà en Provence d'après les autels des âmes du Purgatoire (XVe–XXe s.)* 76. Duplicated and to appear as an article in *Annales, ESC*. M. Agulhon, *Pénitents et Francs-Maçons de l'ancienne Provence* (L'histoire sans frontière) (Paris, 1968).

manuals, books of devotion and so on).[12] Instead of making a clear-cut separation between popular religious culture and religious thought among the *élite*, ought we not to speak rather of reciprocal interchange between the two, as M. Certeau has done for the French seventeenth century?[13] In this way the historian, far from isolating this or that element of the explanation, in the first place puts it back in its context to measure its "credibility" and compares it with all the others, since his purpose is to seek, not to separate, various types of explanation but to discover particular situations, which act as centres of a complex interplay of various influences.

As time goes on, it has become clear that the simple types of sociological explanation are ambivalent. Take the family influences which, since the works of Ph. Aries, the historian is quite ready to recognize as determinant.

Now sociologists themselves,[14] perhaps in the light of the present questionings of youth, point out that a child's religious personality may well be established in the very opposite sense to the influences received. More generally the historian experiences some disquiet at the sight of the sociologist lumping together the various age levels of a population as if it were just a matter of one and the same person, arguing from an attitude adopted at the age of fifteen the probable evolution in behaviour at forty. History has often noted the complete change of attitude in a whole population in the course of just one generation.

Other criteria, also, those, that is, bound up with economic disruption, are equally ambiguous. Of course, religious sociology seems to have established definitively that variations in practice are in direct relationship with income levels and that everywhere religious practice among the working class is less than in the higher classes.[15] But has it also been shown that emigration always

[12] J. Ferté, *La Vie religieuse dans les campagnes parisiennes (1622–1965)* (Paris, 1962). G. Le Bras has always called for the widest possible comparison of the most diverse data, and protested against the confining of religious sociology to the mere statistics of religious practice.

[13] M. de Certeau, "L'Histoire religieuse au 17e siècle, problèmes de méthode", in *Revue des Sciences Religieuses* (April–June, 1969).

[14] H. Carrier, *Psychosociologie de l'appartenance religieuse* (Rome, 1966), pp. 225–6.

[15] E. Pin, *Pratique religieuse et classes sociales dans une paroisse urbaine, St Pothin à Lyon* (Paris, 1956).

works as a factor making for the abandonment of religion? And is this as true of populations on the move like the masons of the Creuse Department or the Corsicans who display greater fidelity than might be thought to their "native" customs, as it is of the regions of Languedoc where the mountain folk take with them a little of the fervour of their native Cevennes? The same observation applies to concentrations in agriculture or in industry: G. Cholvy, and this was also observed by P. Bois, has shown the importance of the idea of the presence on the spot, fortuitous though it is, of the great landowner or important industrialist. And how are we to estimate the spiritual or intellectual factors in the preservation or alteration of religious affiliation such as they are usually accepted, namely, school, the press, sects or societies of free thought? It will be enough to recall G. Cholvy's extraordinarily convergent observations on the impossibility of knowing the exact part played by these factors: their influence emerges as neutral, even the direct opposite of that attributed to them, and the same is true of contact with Protestants or moving to indifferent or less religious parts of the country. These sometimes are the cause of more tightly knit Catholic communities or of those with greater apostolic fervour. At the very least they take us back again to those regional temperaments, those cultural "regions" whose enduring quality has been acknowledged by F. Boulard and J. Rémy as alone compatible with differences of level of religious practice from one place to another and even in centres *a priori* as autonomous as towns are in comparison with their rural environment. In these cases rather it is a matter of symbiosis.

Further, we must be careful to avoid letting this idea of "cultural region" become, like "regional character", some *ultima ratio*, and in fact an irrational concept blocking research. Historical analysis, however, shows a way out; it enables us to discover those stages which have gradually gone to the make-up of a religious mentality—features, originally, of catechesis which through transmission by word of mouth, together with popular myths and iconography, has been a very special factor in the religious life of the parish.[16] Regarding the Languedoc region,

[16] See the last chapters of J. B. Neveux, *Vie spirituelle et vie sociale entre Rhin et Baltique au XVIIe siècle de T. Arndt à P. J. Spener* (Paris, 1967).

Leroy-Ladurée, and following him Cholvy, have emphasized the supporting role in the spread of the Gospel played by language and local dialects.

Religious influences have been largely determined by preaching and missions which form a continuation of catechesis: after Sevrin's study of the question, recent work by Fr Berthelot du Chesnay and L. Perouas for the seventeenth century and Fr Huot-Pleuroux for the nineteenth century, the importance of the reports on internal missions has clearly appeared. This was first pointed out by G. Le Bras.[17]

All these methods of preaching the Gospel take us back in the last place to the theology courses, or, more accurately, to the categories of theology and spirituality taught to young clerics in the seminary courses. L. Perouas concludes his thesis with them. Nothing is more instructive also in this respect than the pastoral work and its effects in the long term, as it was undertaken by the Corsican bishops, and particularly by Alexandre Sauli, in the application of the ordinances of the Tridentine Counter-Reform.[18] But what also emerges from this study is the conjunction between the success of this reform and the profound effect produced by the wars against Genoa under Sampiero Corso—the assertion of Corsican personality and the development of a new religious personality went hand in hand. In addition to theological systems and often in relation to them events have their place; this is what Ch. Marcilhacy called "history's share".

This share assumes such importance that this historical sociology is increasingly bound up with a history of pastoral practice and we might well be justified in making history the normal gauge of sociology.

"Every religious society lives in time", wrote Le Bras. "We cannot solve or even propound its problems without reference to

[17] P. Berthelot du Chesnay, *Les Missions de S. Jean Eudes. Contribution à l'histoire des missions en France au XVIIe siècle*. L. Perouas, *Le diocèse de la Rochelle de 1648 à 1724 sociologie et pastorale* (Paris, 1964). *Mémoires des missions Montfortains dans l'Ouest (1740–1779)* (Poitiers, 1964). P. Huot-Pleuroux, *La vie chrétienne dans le Doubs et la Haute Saône, de 1860 à 1900, d'après les comptes-rendus des missions paroissiales* (Besançon, 1966).

[18] F. J. Casta, *Evêques et curés corses dans la tradition pastorale du Concile de Trente (1570–1620)* (Ajaccio, 1965) (Corse historique, 5th year).

the past.... I regard history as indispensable in the investigation of causes."[19]

The ambivalence of the sociological criteria of "de-christianization" introduces us to a more radical criticism affecting the very processes of sociological thinking applied to religious history, to the extent, it is true, that the latter desires to confine itself to determinism.[20]

It has been pointed out that of all the phenomena appertaining to the history of societies the least flexible of all is the religious factor: the established characteristics of religious fidelity, in varying degrees, are extraordinarily persistent. The differences to be observed between various cultural regions are found again and again in the long term and change only slowly.[21] And yet at the regional level religious practice shows ups and downs of fervour of a short-term nature, a reflection in some sort of important events affecting the social conscience deeply. Ch. Marcilhacy has pointed out in this connection the significance for the Orléans region of the publication of the *Syllabus*. On the other hand, all Church historians have been struck by periods of spiritual renewal, "spiritual waves" for example, occurring in the first half of the seventeenth century, at the French Restoration and in the thirties of this century.[22] And it is no less striking to notice that these revivals have generally occurred in total variance with material and spiritual conditions which, it might have been thought, would have led to the decline of religious fervour. Without mentioning the barbarous state of the French countryside when St Vincent de Paul began to evangelize it, it yet seems true that the whole missionary concept and even religious sociology were derived from the discovery of the real state of de-christianization in which the "eldest daughter of the Church" was labouring. On the other hand, a great number of institutions, an apparent state of ecclesiastical prosperity can very well conceal a real lack of religious fervour. Thus no term appears more ambiguous than

---

[19] In *Traité de sociologie* (Gurvitch), vol. II, p. 93, 3rd edn. (Paris, 1968).
[20] This is rejected by E. Pin, *Essais de sociologie religieuse* (Paris, 1967), p. 261.
[21] Cf. J. Gadille, *La pensée et l'action politique des évêques français au début de la IIIe République, 1870–1883*, vol. I (Paris, 1967), pp. 197–9.
[22] A. Latreille, E. Delaruelle and R. Remond, *Histoire du catholicisme français*, vols. 2 and 3 (Paris, 1960–2).

"Christian success" or "successful Christianity"; Boulard and Rémy referred to this in their last book.[23] Of course they are right to appeal to a religious remedy, but can this latter be expressed merely by comparing a "religious region" with one which shows a lesser degree of religious dispositions. And how far is it right historically to speak of "Christian countries"?[24]

As a matter of fact it seems more accurate to keep in mind the relationship between means of evangelization and culture, in the historic meaning of the term, of a human group. A certain success can be allowed where this relationship is concordant and harmonious, where social life is effectively "informed" by religion; but history gives the impression that far from ever being fixed, a balance of this sort always remains threatened, precarious and continually called in question; and all the more since within the same group religious views are subject to strong variation in accordance with the differences of social strata.[25]

Nevertheless, it would be childish to think that such a critical examination of sociology by religious history means that the outlook and methods of the two disciplines must remain foreign to each other. The opposite is true and it is rather their complementary nature that should emerge.[26]

Religious history has been confined for too long to the study of the special case, to the *élite*, the hero and the saint, losing sight of the necessary basis of any ecclesiastical life provided by popular piety and the humblest forms of religious commitment.

In this way the history of the Churches has been confused with that of their spiritual leaders, with the position adopted by them in the pulpit or in the press. By leaving out of account the very powerful pressure exerted by the spiritual needs and the general views of the masses there is a risk of giving an untrue picture of the reality. G. Cholvy deals thus with the prevailing state of habitual tensions between teachers and parish priests at the beginning of this century, by means of precise statistics which prove

[23] *Pratique urbaine, op. cit.*, pp. 111, 118.
[24] Cf. L. Perouas, "Contrastes régionaux au XVIIe siècle dans le diocèse de la Rochelle", in *Archives de sociologie des religions*, 15 (1963), p. 121.
[25] H. Carrier, E. Pin, *Essais de sociologie religieuse*, pp. 105-123.
[26] E. Passerin d'Entreves, "Sociologia e Storia religiosa", in *Sociologica*, I (1968), pp. 151-62.

that relations of mutual esteem were more widespread than those of distrust, and this in a part of the country well known for its fierce antagonisms. Enumerations, followed by the full use of all the statistical data to be discovered from those dormant masses whom the Church regards as a precious patrimony, form for the historian the first step of mere intellectual honesty. No religious history in the ordinary sense of the term can do without it at the present time, and sociology has already rendered it an immense service by drawing its attention to the valuable source of information to be found in the reports of missions, pastoral visits or just the ordinary parochial registers.

But it is not going far enough to state that sociology constitutes the primary support of religious history. Having already opportunely reminded the latter of the popular sources of religion, sociological analyses bring it back to what should have been its fundamental objective, that is, the religious expression of the ideas determined for itself by a special group rather than the history of the ecclesiastical institution dealt with for its own sake. At several points of his last book H. Carrier reminds us how few forms of conduct are as "comprehensive" as religious behaviour and what an instrument of social synthesis is to be found in the religious experience.

We know what light this sociological outlook has enabled E. Poulat to throw on the history of the priest-workers, modernism and integrism. H. Carrier concludes his work with Polybius's formula, *Religio praecipuum humanae societatis vinculum.*[27] How wonderful it would be to try to do for religions and societies of the Christian era what Fustel brought about in his *Cité antique*! There would then be no longer religious history but only the history of religious societies. Far from history taking the place of sociology, it is for the latter to make use of history for its own purposes. It should not thereby see the religious phenomenon as merely the expression of social needs, and confined to a sort of pathology of the sacred, exhibiting religious manifestations exclusively as the outlet for obscure revolts or unconscious social conflicts. Rather would sociology show how, in the history of a social body, religious expressions and institutions have gradually

[27] H. Carrier, *Psychosociologie de l'appartenance religieuse*, p. 269.

taken shape to answer more adequately specific religious needs through the ever-changing forms of its evolution. Adopting again the idea of "cultural region" which it rediscovered, it would require of history to show how this or that culture assimilated the Gospel message to the extent of identification with it and, on the other hand, why another culture has rejected it.

Far from remaining indifferent and, still less, strangers to each other, religious sociology and religious history would then be fused together in a more exacting and loftier form of explanation.

Translated by Lancelot Sheppard

PART III
DOCUMENTATION
CONCILIUM

Concilium General Secretariat

Theology at the Universities

AS institutions for ecclesiastical training, university theological
faculties are finding themselves in an increasingly difficult position.

With the exception of Poland there has been a decline everywhere in the number of students wishing to prepare themselves
for the ministry. This can be attributed in large part to the uncertainty which surrounds the ecclesiastical image of the minister
so that many students shy away from any undertaking that ties
them to the institutional Church.[1]

On the other hand, the number of students who study theology simply because they are interested is on the increase. Such
students tend to look towards theology to find a viable philosophy
of life.

This increasingly lay approach to theology is particularly prominent in the United States, in German-speaking countries and in
the Netherlands,[2] that is, in those countries which are running
ahead of developments in the institutional Church.

Moreover, there is hardly a university in the world where the

[1] See H. Thielicke, *Uber die Angst des heutigen Theologiestudenten vor
dem geistlichen Amt.* Sammlung gemeinverständlicher Vorträge und
Schriften aus dem Gebiet der Theologie und Religionsgeschichte (Tübingen, 1967), p. 247.
[2] Cf. H. Schuster, "Die Chance der Laientheologen," in *Diakonia/Der
Seelsorger* 1 (1970, 2), pp. 73 f.; H. Pompey and J. Dirnbeck, "Aufgaben
für Laientheologen," *ibid.*, pp. 118-24; C. Ellis Nelson, "Church Education and the Teaching of Religion in the Public Domain," in *Theological
Education* III, 2 (Winter, 1967), pp. 384-95.

faculty of theology has not become a hot-bed of permanent un-
rest. This phenomenon can be observed in all denominations in
South and North America, Italy, Holland, France, Germany,
Spain, Africa, etc. Discussion and protest flourish everywhere.[3]

The debate centres around questions such as: How can we
adjust the study of theology to the practical needs of our age?
What really is theology? What should theology be studying in
the twentieth century? Considering the way in which we understand science today, can we still say that there is room for a
faculty of theology in a university? Should we not admit that
theological faculties are out of date and is it not then the task
of theologians to expose the irrelevancy of theology and Churches,
and ultimately to liquidate them?

One often finds an attitude of resignation among the teaching
staff with regard to these issues brought up by the students.[4]
Could we not rather see in all this a proof of the vitality of the
theological faculty since it has brought theology once again to
the fore in the debates that constitute the life of a university?

The increasing unrest in these faculties has several causes, and
these are partly connected with the historical relationship of a
faculty with a particular university, partly with the changes in
the world of science, and partly with the social situation of the
Church.

In the first section of this documentation we shall survey the
history of theological faculties in the light of recent studies in
order to arrive at a better understanding of the present difficulties. The second will deal with some new approaches and point
to some new developments in Africa. We may then, perhaps,
discover one or two possible ways of overcoming the current
crisis.

[3] A documentation on protest action by Evangelical theological students
in Germany appeared in *Theologiestudenten 1969*, publ. by Evangelisches
Verlagswerk (Stuttgart, 1969). A survey of this contestation among Catholic theologians was published by Ben van Onna and M. Stankowski in
Kritischer Katholizismus. Argumente gegen die Kirchen-Gesellschaft
(Fischer: Frankfurt/Hamburg, 1969). See also the issue, "Student en kerk,"
of the review *Tegenspraak* (1970).

[4] This is the situation in the colleges described by C. Gestrich, in his
"Zutrauen zur Theologie. Eine Besinnung über Theologiestudium und
kirchliches Amt," in *Evang. Kommentare* 3 (March, 1970), pp. 139-44.

The Development of Theological Faculties

In this context the word *facultas* corresponded more or less to our modern "profession", and so the various faculties of a university provided a training for various professions.[5] Towards the end of the twelfth century there arose a new corporation in Paris, Bologna, Oxford and Cambridge, and the name first given to it in Paris[6] was *"universitas magistrorum et scholarium"* (university of masters and scholars).

This association was organized in four faculties, three higher ones (theology, law and medicine) and the fourth, a lower one, covering the arts and usually divided into four nationalities. The university took shape at a time when Europe enjoyed a period of economic prosperity.

During the twelfth century new methods were developed for theology, law, medicine and philosophy, with which the monastic and cathedral schools could no longer cope. At the same time higher standards were required for the training of the more important ecclesiastical, imperial and royal officials.[7]

The university was in those days practically the only centre for education and research, so that we may speak here of a monopoly. The constitution fixed the educational programme, the division of the academic year and the granting of the licence to teach.

A theological student in Paris would have to follow a five-year course in the faculty of arts before he could be admitted to the

[5] R. Meister, "Beiträge zur Gründungsgeschichte der mittelalterlichen Universität," in *Anzeiger der phil.-hist. Klasse der Oesterr. Akademie der Wissenschaften* 4 (Vienna, 1957), p. 37.

[6] Research on these origins has been surveyed by H. Schmidinger in "Zur Entstehung der Universität im Mittelalter," in *Forschung und Bildung. Aufgaben einer katholischer Universität* (Fribourg, 1965), pp. 127–141. For the history of particular universities use has been made of S. d'Irsay, *Histoire des Universités françaises et étrangères des origines à nos jours*, 2 vols. (Paris, 1933–5); the new ed. by F. M. Powicke and H. B. Emden of H. Rashdall's *The Universities of Europe in the Middle Ages*, 3 vols. (Oxford, 1936); A. Franzen, art. "Universitäten" in *Lex. f. Theol. u. Kirche*, X (2nd ed., 1965), pp. 510–7; L. Petry, art. "Universität" (historisch), in *Religion in Gesch. u. Gegenwart* VI (3rd ed., 1962), pp. 1165–1170.

[7] Cf. P. Classen, "Die Hohen Schulen und die Geselschaft im 12. Jahrhundert," in *Nachrichten der Giessener Hochschulgesellschaft* 33 (1964), pp. 145–57.

eight-year course of theology. In the theological faculty the first four years were spent on the study of Scripture, after which the rest was given to the study of the four books of *Sententiae* of Peter Lombard.[8]

Few students managed to stay the course and reach the doctorate. Most of them left before the end and took up some office. They were trained in the scholastic method.

This scholastic method proceeded in four stages: (1) the reading of a text (*lectio*); (2) the setting up of a problem (*quaestio*); (3) the discussion of the problem (*disputatio*), and (4) the solution of the problem (*determinatio*).[9] The upsurge of theology in the thirteenth century cannot be explained without the rediscovery of Aristotle. His work provided the material for a genuine scientific, i.e., methodical investigation and set new standards.

The acceptance of Aristotelian thought in theology led to fierce conflicts,[10] but ended in the synthesis created by Thomas Aquinas, who embodied philosophy in the "sacred doctrine". According to him, philosophy has three functions in the explanation of the faith: it must provide the introduction to the faith (*preambula fidei*), illustrate the content of the faith by analogy and deal with the objections to the faith.[11] And, basically, this also provided the intellectual justification of the place of theology and the presence of a theological faculty in a university.

The further development of the university was profoundly influenced by the fact that, guided by the texts of the ancients, people learned to think systematically. New intellectual discoveries were based on assimilating the contents of books, not on experimenting. The main argument was that of authority.

Nevertheless, the scholastics interpreted these "authorities" very freely—one might almost say that they "manipulated" them.[12] Every year there were also public disputations on a freely chosen topic. At this time scholasticism can hardly be said to have become set in its ways.

[8] J. Le Goff, *Das Hochmittelalter. Fischer Feltgeschichte* XI (Frankfurt/ Hamburg, 1965), pp. 256.   [9] *Ibid.*, p. 258.
[10] Cf. M. D. Chenu, *La Théologie comme science au XIIIe siècle* (3rd ed., Paris, 1957), pp. 67–92.   [11] *Ibid.*, pp. 88 f.
[12] The meaning of *"Auctoritates"* has been extensively examined by M. D. Chenu in *La Théologie au douzième siècle.* Etudes de Philosophie médiévale XLV (2nd ed., Paris, 1966), pp. 353–65.

The centre of theological academic life was the University of Paris. Practically all the famous theologians studied and taught there. This university only lost its prominence in the Hundred Years War with England, when many professors and students went elsewhere.[13]

The popes in Avignon obstructed the setting up of theological faculties in the new universities of Cracow (1364), Vienna (1365) and Pécs-Fünfkirchen (1367). The reason for this may have been the wish to support Paris, a fear of new heresies springing up or also the jealousy of Prague University (1348).[14] In any case, there were several centres of theological studies in Europe by the end of the fourteenth century.

There is not much point in dealing here with the conflicts that opposed one school to another, but it is important to draw attention to the ways in which the theologians were concerned about the good of the Church. It is enough to mention the work of theologians like John Wycliffe and John Huss, who wanted the Church to return to her biblical origins.

The influence of the theologians reached its peak at the time of the schism. Paris University, and of course particularly its theologians, were for ending the schism and demanded a Council.

The Council of Constance was a triumph for the theologians.[15] There John Gerson defended the supremacy of the Council over the Pope and the deposition of a pope when convicted of heresy or simony. But he began by proving his orthodoxy by declaring that John Huss was guilty of heresy.[16] In this way he wanted to make it clear that the conciliarists should not be confused with heretics but were aware of their responsibility for the purity of the Church's doctrine. Unfortunately, the Council of Constance

[13] The situation at Paris University has been described by A. G. Weiler in *Heinrich von Gorkum (d. 1431). Seine Stellung in der Philosophie und der Theologie des Spätmittelalters* (Hilversum/Cologne, 1962), pp. 17–38. Heinrich von Gorkum studied and taught there from 1395–1419, after which he went to Cologne University.

[14] Cf. R. Meister, *op. cit.*, pp. 43–6.

[15] Cf. A. Franzen, "Das Konzil der Einheit. Einigungsbemühungen und konziliare Gedanken auf dem Konstanzer Konzil. Die Dekrete *Haec sancta* und *Frequens*," in *Das Konzil von Konstanz. Beiträge zu seiner Geschichte und Theologie* (Freiburg, 1964), pp. 69–112.

[16] Cf. P. De Vooght, "Jean Huss et ses juges," *ibid.*, pp. 152–73.

did not bring about a reform of the Church in her head and in her members.

We are much less well informed about the universities in the age of humanism and the Renaissance than at their origin. To help remedy this the Historical Institute of the University of Geneva published some documents and studies.[17]

The general opinion used to be that there was little change in the life of the universities up to the seventeenth and eighteenth centuries:[18] the medieval statutes, the pyramid structure of the faculties, the corporations, examinations, academic degrees and diplomas were all maintained. This was accompanied by some symptoms of decline: a clinging to the traditional scholastic system and teaching methods, and a running down of the financial resources.

The social background of the students changed. The image of the poor student disappeared because the grants diminished and the Church no longer felt herself capable of providing places for those who finished their training at a university. Thus the university became the preserve of the aristocracy and the middle class. The humanists fiercely attacked the universities for their rigid and unscientific character, even though they themselves had been trained there.

A genuine renewal set in, mainly inspired by the colleges which were founded in large numbers in the fifteenth and sixteenth centuries.[19] Students studied in classes and the lectures given in such colleges became lectures in the modern sense of the word.

Here the humanists spread their ideas and taught the classical languages and classical literature. The tradition of these "colleges" has been preserved in Oxford and Cambridge up to the present day.

The most famous is the *collegium trilingue* (trilingual college),[20] which Erasmus of Rotterdam helped to found in Louvain.

---

[17] *Les Universités Européennes du XIVe au XVIIIe siècle. Actes du Colloque International à l'occasion du VIe Centenaire de l'Université Jagellone de Cracovie 6–8 Mai 1964* (Geneva, 1967).

[18] S. Stelling-Michaud tried to correct this view in "Quelques Remarques sur l'Histoire des Universités à l'époque de la Renaissance," *ibid.*, pp. 78 f.

[19] *Ibid.*, pp. 79 f.

[20] H. De Vocht, *History of the Foundation and the Rise of the Collegium*

This became the model for the Collège de France, and influenced the Spanish universities of the Golden Age. Calvin, Ignatius of Loyola, Guillaume Farel and Francis Xavier all studied in such colleges in Paris. It is therefore hardly surprising that the *ratio studiorum* of the Society of Jesus and the *Ordre du Collège* of Calvin have so much in common.[21]

The most striking example of Erasmus's Christian humanism was embodied in the University of Alcalá[22] (founded in 1526). Here Cardinal Cisneros de Henares created a new university, free from inquisitorial pressures and no longer tied to the apron strings of the antiquated scholasticism of Salamanca.

Here theology became the backbone of the university but was no longer limited to dogmatic theology. The teaching of the biblical languages flourished. Thomism, Scotism and nominalism were all represented. The aim was to create an atmosphere of intellectual freedom and to train and form the students into genuine Europeans. The function of the theological faculty was no longer taken to be to train priests but to give a Christian formation. One of their star students was Juan Luis Vives who was later to teach in Oxford and Paris.

The movements of the Reformation and the Counter-Reformation had a decisive influence on the theological faculties.[23] Luther occupied a dominant position in the University of Wittenberg. It was while lecturing at the university that he developed his views on the reform of the Church and gathered students around him who then spread his teaching throughout Germany and Northern Europe. For some years Wittenberg became as important as Rome and Paris.

In his own life Luther built up a new image of the pastor which is still alive today. For him the pastor is a scholar (*doctus*) who has studied at a university, is married and is an ordinary citizen.

Trilingue Lovaniense, 1517–1550 (Univ. de Louvain. Recueil des Travaux d'Histoire et de Philologie, 3rd ser., 42, 4th ser., 4–5, 10, Louvain, 1951–1955), 4 vols.   [21] S. Stelling-Michaud, *op. cit.*, p. 80.
[22] Cf. for what follows M. Bataillon, *Erasmo y España* (2nd ed., Mexico, 1966), pp. 22–72; 154–66; 339–61; 699–705.
[23] L. Petry, "Die Reformation als Epoche der deutschen Universitätsgeschichte," in *Glaube und Geschichte*. Festgabe Joseph Lortz, II (Baden-Baden, 1958), p. 327.

Most German universities were on the side of the old Church and were partly forced to subscribe to the Reformation. Melanchthon had the idea of a university where reform and humanism would go hand in hand.[24] A comparative study of the theology taught to the generations that followed shows that orthodox Protestant theology and the theology of the Jesuits had much in common. Both fell victim to the scholastic method. When there were doctrinal conflicts within one camp, as happened in the controversy between Jansenists and Jesuits in France, the arguments ground to a standstill and one can fairly speak of the loss of a sense of realism in dogmatic theology.

While in the sixteenth century the theological faculties were still consulted by Church or State on important points, as happened, for instance, with Wittenberg or with the theological congregations of Trent which thoroughly discussed the conciliar decrees before they were passed, afterwards their influence dwindled to a minimum. Trent reformed the training for the priesthood in the Catholic Church from ground level by ordering the creation of seminaries for all dioceses.[25]

These seminaries for the priesthood, mainly run by Jesuits, were to give the future clergy a better formation than before in order to be the better equipped to compete with Protestant ministers. The study arrangements seem to have differed very little from those of the Jesuits themselves.

The situation of the universities in the seventeenth century deteriorated seriously. Scientific discoveries and the new thinking in philosophy found no recognition there, and they continued their existence on the periphery of the intellectual life of that period. But at the end of this century the jurist Thomasius opened up new perspectives at the then recently founded University of Halle (1694).

The new intellectual stimulus spread from the study of law to the various branches of knowledge. Legal documents were

[24] Cf. M. Steinmetz, "Die Konzeption der deutschen Universitäten im Zeitalter von Humanismus und Reformation," in *Les Universités Européennes*, pp. 114-27, esp. 121 ff.
[25] Cf. H. Jedin, "Das Leitbild des Priesters nach dem Tridentinum und dem Vaticanum II," in *Theologie und Glaube* 60 (1970, 2), pp. 102-24.

brought out and investigated, and this led to the attempt at developing new methods in the study of history. At the founding of the University of Göttingen (1737) Freiherr von Münchhausen was inspired by the views of Thomasius: "Science must form men who are useful in the world."[26]

The statutes of the theological faculty were by and large moulded on the ideas of L. Mosheim, a theologian of Helmstedt who wanted theology to steer a middle course between orthodoxy, deism and naturalism.[27] The members of the faculty were forbidden by statute to exercise any kind of censorship over publications of medicine, law and philosophy, or to accuse colleagues of other faculties of heresy. Moreover, the theologians were told not to attack each other or bring each other into disrepute. This was not meant to reduce their work to nondescript platitudes but rather to check the kind of controversy that prevailed in the seventeenth century. The dogmatic basis was still provided by the confessional books of the Evangelical Church but systematic theology turned to history. Students should not merely become learned but also be prepared for pastoral work.

A few years later von Münchhausen founded the Academy of Science in Göttingen.[28] His purpose was to reintroduce research into the university whose task he saw as a combination of research and learning, and he wanted to create the conditions that would make this possible.

The example of Göttingen was widely followed elsewhere, as, for instance in Berlin University, founded in 1810.[29] This university went further and linked the practical set-up of Göttingen with Fichte's ideas about science and romantic ideas on education.

Here idealist philosophy inspired the whole concept of the university as the *universitas litterarum*. Schleiermacher, the first

---

[26] Götz von Selle, *Universität Göttingen. Wesen und Geschichte* (Göttingen, 1953), p. 26.   [27] *Ibid.*, pp. 19 f.
[28] For the statutes of the theological faculty of Göttingen, see *ibid.*, p. 40.
[29] For the foundation of Berlin University W. Weischedel's *Idee und Wirklichkeit einer Universität. Dokumente zur Geschichte der Friedrich-Wilhelms-Universität zu Berlin* (Berlin, 1960) is most useful. See particularly the introduction by W. Weischedel (pp. xi–xxxiv) and the projects put forward by J. G. Fichte (pp. 30–105) and F. D. Schleiermacher (pp. 106–92).

theologian of Berlin University, tried to assign the place of theology within the context of the other sciences[30] but was basically still too much influenced by the views of Fichte. His disciples were still orthodox and loyal to the Church.

The year 1773 saw the suppression of the Jesuits, which led to profound changes in the Catholic universities, because by then the Order controlled practically the whole educational system in Catholic Europe, and now had to abandon that position. During the 250 years of its existence it had failed to adapt its programme of studies to the new developments, particularly in the field of history.

Under Maria Theresa and Joseph II the study of theology underwent a far-reaching reform.[31] Restrictions were put on speculative theology while practical and historical theology was explicitly required. The whole study of theology was made to aim at pastoral practice. An attempt was made to catch up with the advance made in the teaching of history in the Protestant universities.

In 1774 Rautenstrauch planned a five-year course for theology. The first two years should cover the introductory subjects: general theological knowledge ("encyclopaedia"), Church history, hermeneutics, patrology and the history of theological literature. This was followed by the strictly theological subjects: dogma, moral theology, canon law and, for practical theology, pastoral theology and apologetics (controversy). Other subjects accompanied this study: archaeology, biblical geography, history of religion, history of dogma, history of heresies, the study of the decretals, symbolism, liturgy, catechetics and homiletics.[32] The State forced this reform through because it had a vital interest in a well-trained clergy.[33] This renewal was, however, slow in get-

[30] See the long introduction to *Der christliche Glaube*, where the ideas are put together in the context of the principles of the Evangelical Church (2nd ed., 1830–1).
[31] See E. Winter, *Der Josephinismus und seine Geschichte* (1943).
[32] E. C. Scherer, *Geschichte und Kirchengeschichte an den deutschen Universitäten. Ihre Anfänge im Zeitalter des Humanismus und ihre Ausbildung zu selbständigen Disziplinen* (Freiburg i. Br., 1927), pp. 399 f.
[33] Kant described the function of the faculties as follows: "According to reason (i.e., objectively) the motivating forces which the government can use for its purpose (to influence the people) should be placed in the follow-

ting off the ground for the simple reason that there was a shortage of properly qualified staff.

It was not until the beginning of the nineteenth century that Catholic theology can be said to have caught up academically with Protestant theology. For instance, the Catholic theologians of Tübingen[34] were then as familiar with the philosophy of idealism and historical research as their Protestant colleagues. Some of these theologians also showed a certain concern about the reform of the Church, as evidenced by J. B. Hirsher's *Die kirchlichen Zustände der Gegenwart* (1849—The situation of the Church today).[35] But the time was not yet ripe for the implementation of his suggestions.

There is a tendency to speak of a philosophical and artistic decline after Hegel's death in 1831. The failure of the various revolutions of 1848 led to a reactionary backlash in political and intellectual life. The Industrial Revolution created a proletariat of the masses in the towns, and this proletariat drifted away from the sphere of ecclesiastical influence. The clergy was seen to belong to a "better" class and had little understanding of what went on in society. Moreover, the natural sciences began to dominate in the universities, and science was no longer seen in the terms of idealism but of positivism. This in turn changed the approach to the arts. Atheistic philosophy and the results of the historical criticism of the New Testament[36] spread among large sectors of the people and began to alienate the intellectuals from the Church.

The Churches and their theologians saw themselves besieged

---

ing order: first any lasting good, then the civic good of man as member of society, and finally the bodily good (long life and good health)": *Der Streit der Fakultäten*, Weischedel's edition VI (1964), p. 283. "A university must have a philosophical faculty. In view of the three points mentioned above this faculty should control these forces since all depends on the truth; the usefulness which the government expects of the higher faculties is, however, only of secondary importance" (*ibid.*, p. 290).

[34] T. M. Schoof, *Aggiornamento. De doorbraak van een nieuwe katholieke theologie* (Baarn, 1968), pp. 30 f., with bibliography on pp. 50 f. The *Theologische Quartalschrift* has devoted the first issue of its 150th year to an exposé of its own purpose and has given brief biographies of the professors who taught at the Catholic theological faculty of Tübingen.

[35] *Ibid.*, pp. 35–9.

[36] In 1835 D. F. Strauss published his *Das Leben Jesu*.

on every side and sought shelter in their traditions. In the Protestant Churches a confessionalism became prevalent which, like the orthodoxy of the Enlightenment, avoided any confrontation with scriptural criticism. Typical of this negative attitude was the book by the Dutch revivalist Isaac da Costa, *Objections to the spirit of this century* (1823).[37]

In spite of this the theological faculties of the Dutch universities taught a liberal theology and scriptural criticism. Because of this a "free university" was founded in Amsterdam in 1880, based on the principles of the Reformation. The founders left the "Hervormde Kerk" in 1886 and set up the "Gereformeerde Kerk".[38]

Similar tendencies developed in the Catholic Church. The theology of the Tübingen school dwindled into oblivion. Attempts to face the spirit of the age were effectively squashed in 1864 by the encyclical *Quanta Cura* and the Syllabus of Errors.[39]

Thanks to papal support and the influence of the Jesuits at the Gregorianum in Rome neo-scholasticism became the dominant trend in a relatively short time. The intellectual dependence on this Roman theology was reinforced by Vatican I. The way in which this school of theology saw itself is well expressed in the titles of the two main works by J. Kleutgens, s.j., *The Theology of the past* and *The Philosophy of the past*.[40]

Before passing on to the turn of the century we must mention the foundation of *Catholic universities*. In 1833 the Belgian bishops set up a *Universitas Studiorum* in Malines, which was transferred to Louvain in 1835 in order to maintain the traditions of Louvain University.[41] This university was meant to enable Catholics to acquire higher education and at the same time

---

[37] I. da Costa, *Bezwaren tegen den geest der eeuw*, new edition in *Vrijmoedige Bedenkingen*, Spectrum van de Nederlandse Letterkunde 20 (Utrecht-Antwerp, 1968), pp. 123–88.

[38] Cf. T. L. Haitjema, *De nieuwere geschiedenis van Neerlands Kerk der Hervorming* (The Hague, 1964), pp. 223–80.

[39] See Alec R. Vidler, *The Church in an Age of Revolution* (Pelican History of the Church 5, 1961), p. 151.

[40] For the Roman school, see W. Kaspers, *Die Lehre von der Tradition in der Römischen Schule* (Die Uberlieferung in der neueren Theologie, vol. V, Freiburg i. Br., 1962).

[41] L. van der Essen, *De Universiteit te Leuven. Haar ontstaan, haar geschiedenis, haar organisatie, 1425-1953* (Louvain, n.d.).

to protect them against the dangerous teachings of the State universities. This example was followed elsewhere. A number of Catholic universities were founded in North America during the 1840s. In 1875/6 the Institut Catholique was founded in Paris and similar Catholic Institutes of Higher Education were set up in Toulouse, Angers, Lyons and Lille. A university was erected in Fribourg (Switzerland)[42] in 1890, and finally the Catholic University of Nijmegen (Holland) followed in 1923.[43]

With a few exceptions dogmatic theology became a rigid system which was satisfied with the repetition of pronouncements by the magisterium and conciliar texts. The only field where methodical and creative work was still undertaken was history, and even there within narrow limits.

Because he embodied modern criticism in his defence of the Catholic position against Harnack's *History of Dogma*, Loisy was condemned. Modernism was deemed heretical in one sweeping condemnation, and all clergy were compelled to take the anti-Modernist oath in 1910.

Theologians were subjected to a real reign of terror which eased off only gradually under the popes who succeeded Pius X.[44]

It is therefore hardly astonishing that the leading theologians of the first half of the twentieth century were to be found in the Protestant camp: Karl Barth, Rudolf Bultmann and Paul Tillich.

Towards the end of the nineteenth century the theological faculties in general were enlivened by the debate on their attitude to comparative religion and its ancillary disciplines, a debate which could still have its relevance today. In the Netherlands the tendency was to replace the faculty of theology by one of comparative religion. Adolf Harnack[45] rejected this on the

[42] For its origins see R. Ruffieux, "Freiburg und die Universität," in *Forschung und Bildung*, etc., pp. 167–88.
[43] For the question of the Catholic University, see J. H. Newman, *The Idea of a University* (New York/London/Toronto, 1947); J. H. Walgrave, "J. H. Newman und das Problem der katholischen Universität," in *Forschung und Bildung*, etc., pp. 142–66; N. A. Luyten, "Warum katholische Universität?" *ibid.*, pp. 13–34; E. Schillebeeckx, "Die katholische Universität als Problem und Verheissung," *ibid.*, pp. 35–51.
[44] A. R. Vidler, *op. cit.*, pp. 83–9.
[45] "Die Aufgabe der theologischen Fakultäten und die allgemeine Religionsgeschichte, nebst einem Nachwort (1901)," in *Reden und Aufsätze* II (Giessen, 1904), pp. 159–87.

ground of practical difficulties: there were no qualified lecturers and one could just as well study all religions as an accompaniment to the history of the Christian religion (p. 168). The historical method is the only one that would suit a systematic treatment of theology (p. 166).

This cultural Protestantism of Harnack's left no room for the Christian faith and its claim to absolute relevancy. Dialectic theology reacted fiercely to this watering down of Christian theology because it denied any connection between religion and the Christian faith and saw in religion only a kind of self-glorification of man. But by its sharp reaction dialectic theology cut itself off from the other sciences and really put itself outside the university.

To sum up, theology was divided into the various disciplines as we know them today in the age of Enlightenment. It failed to incorporate scriptural criticism in a positive way. Those theologians that adopted the scientific trends of their age became alienated from their Church.

New Ways and Fresh Attempts

In its Decree on the training of the clergy, *Optatam totius*, Vatican II provided for a modernization of the study of theology. An introduction to theology is considered necessary and a better integration of philosophy and theology is required. Contemporary developments must be seriously studied and theology must take its cue from the renewal movement as expressed in the Council (nn. 14 and 15). Adjustment to local conditions and situations is left to the bishops.

In March 1970 the Congregation for Education published a new instruction with guidelines for the training of the clergy.[46] This instruction was meant to serve as a norm for the national Episcopal Conferences which are charged with applying the Decree to their local and temporal situations. This instruction does not really go beyond what the Decree has already stipulated. It contains no detailed projects and merely insists on the adjustment of practical decisions to pastoral training.

[46] See *Herder-Korrespondenz* 24 (1970, 5), pp. 213-7.

In Germany[47] the Evangelical professional bodies submitted their own plan for the reform of the study of theology which asked for better structures than in the past. Philosophy and the study of Scripture are put at the beginning of the course, to be followed by an even distribution of the various strictly theological disciplines and practical exercises during the holidays in preparation for the ministry.

In 1968 the German bishops published the details of a reorganization of theology for candidates for the priesthood. Their proposals have been critically examined by Karl Rahner.[48] According to him, these proposals do not really correct the faults of the prevailing system. They suffer, particularly, from a lack of concern for philosophy and from a fragmentation of energy over too many subjects, which hinder a clear view of what theology is about. Instead, he proposes a basic study which picks up the questions of the students, deals with them philosophically and then proceeds to treat them theologically. In this way the main impact of the studies is directed to systematic theology in a way which keeps in touch with philosophy and incorporates the historical subjects.

This idea of Rahner's is put into practice principally by the higher educational institutes of the religious orders.[49] They have a basic course in theology and have so far been successful. The level of this introduction is in general very high, but it appears that it is very difficult to maintain this high level during the rest of the course. In spite of this there is a determination to continue on these lines.

The papal university of the Gregorianum has produced a detailed programme of studies and a reform of its statutes. This is the fruit of co-operation between lecturers and students.[50] According to these new statutes the direction of the theological faculty is a matter of participation, involving students and staff.

[47] *Theologiestudium. Entwurf einer Reform*, prepared by W. Herrmann and G. Lautner (Munich, 1965).

[48] Karl Rahner, "Zur Neuordnung der theologischen Studien", in *Stimmen der Zeit* 181 (1968), pp. 1–21, an expansion of his "Zur Reform des Theologie-studiums," in *Quaestiones disputatae* 41 (Freiburg i. Br., 1969).

[49] Cf. G. Muschalek's report, "Studienreform an den Ordenshochschulen der Bundesrepublik," in *Stimmen der Zeit* 185 (1970, 6), pp. 406–20.

[50] Cf. F. A. Sullivan, "A Report on the Reform of the Faculty of Theology

In so far as the reform of the programme of studies is concerned, the first question asked was what the real task of the faculty should be. Here the faculty was sharply distinguished from the seminary. The faculty should prepare students for lecturing later on and for pastoral work among intellectuals, and should enable them to pursue their own researches.

One has the impression that this aim could not be achieved under the existing system (two years' philosophy and four years' theology, leading to the licentiate) (p. 848).

The new programme provides for a two-year course in philosophy and a three-year course of basic study (*Grundstudium*), to be rounded off by an examination for the baccalaureate. After this one can follow one year of practical training.

Only above-average students are admitted to the two-year course which leads to the licentiate. They must specialize in one main branch of theology, after which they can prepare themselves for their degree (p. 849).

The "basic study" contains lectures, exercises and seminars for small groups. This three-year course deals with theology under three main headings: Christ, the fullness of revelation; the Church, sacrament of Christ, and Man in Christ (pp. 853–6).

According to Rahner such a course gives no separate introduction into the study of the Christian faith and no change is made in the individual branches of theology. It seems to us that this specialization of theological formation is aimed at the future.

The experiments with what are called "contact studies" for parish priests in Western Germany seem to be leading to greater variety in what the theological faculty has to offer in the way of training.[51] There is also a tendency to combine theology with other disciplines, such as sociology, psychology, philology, law, etc.[52] This means the faculty no longer aims exclusively at the

at the Gregorian University," in *Gregorianum* 50/3–4 (1969), pp. 839–58. The same issue contains discussions about the various theological disciplines.

[51] H. M. Müller, "Die Väter studieren wieder. Göttinger Erfahrungen mit Kontaktstudium für Pfarrer," in *Luth. Monatshefte* 9 (1970, 3), pp. 117–9. Cf. E. Bethge, "Pfarrerweiterbildung in den USA," in *Wissenschaft und Praxis in Kirche und in Gesellschaft* 59 (1970, 1), pp. 57–64.
[52] See note 2.

formation of the clergy. It is also likely that the clergy of the future will go in greater numbers to educational institutions that are not universities.[53]

A new situation is developing in the State universities of North America. Until recently these had no theological faculty nor a programme for the study of theology. In recent years, however, one university after another has been offering a course in theology or religion. There is a wide demand for it among the students. It is already said that the State universities have taken over the function of providing a more scientific study of theology while the private ecclesiastical colleges concentrate on the formation of the clergy and the requirements of the practical ministry.

H. W. Turner[54] has gathered some information about recent developments in tropical Africa. Since World War II thirteen universities or university colleges have been set up in what used to be the English-speaking colonies. Practically all these establishments offer the opportunity to study theology or religion in general. This cannot be explained as a left-over from the colonial establishment since among the new universities in Britain itself only one or two offer theology as a subject.

Turner attributes this introduction of religious studies into the African State universities to the fact that religion plays an important part in African life and to the strength of the Christian communities in the new independent States (p. 114). In countries like Sierra Leone, Nigeria and East Africa there are large Christian and Islamic communities, which has led some universities to offer parallel courses in Christian and Islamic theology. The University of Nigeria has, for instance, one course based on the Bible and another on the Koran, and has added a course on the study of religion. The course is then subdivided according to the traditions of the various religious communities (p. 116).

Finally, Turner answers the question whether the religious communities need such a study of theology at university level by

[53] P. Beyerhaus, "Mehr Wege zum Pfarramt. Brauchen wir schon wieder kirchliche Hochschulen?" in *Luth. Monatshefte* 9 (1970, 1), pp. 7–9, has drawn attention to this tendency.

[54] H. W. Turner, "Theology and University from an African Perspective," in *Zeitschr. f. Religions—und Geistesgeschichte* XIX (1967), pp. 114–126.

pointing out that every sector of national life needs the contribution of the university in order to maintain contact with the other sciences and to make study and research possible. On the other hand, in the university theology is a science in its own right which must not be confused with sociology or psychology, and also functions as a force for integration. Moreover, like the other sciences, it has to concern itself with the preservation of freedom (pp. 118–21).

At the beginning of this documentation we spoke of a crisis in the faculty of theology. This crisis is likely to last for some years, just as the crisis in the universities, and the more so since it is only beginning to develop a new self-awareness and is still far from having found all the answers to the questions with which the past has burdened it. The question of the scientific character of theology, for instance, is still unsolved. Nor are we clear about the relationship between theology and the Church(es).

We shall only reach an understanding of, and with, radical groups when theology has achieved a sound methodical approach to its object, the basic questions of God and man within the framework of revelation, and can attempt an explanation of all this in the context of the results of the many analytical studies of modern society. What is now called "political theology" seems to be going this way.

Biographical Notes

GIUSEPPE ALBERIGO, born 21 January 1926, in Varese (Italy). He studied at the University of Milan. He holds a doctorate in jurisprudence (1948) and since 1965 has been a Professor at the Faculty of Political Sciences at the University of Bologna and Director of the Institute of Religious Studies in Bologna. His published work includes *Vescovi italiani al Concilio di Trento* (Florence, 1959) and *Lo sviluppo della dottrina sui poteri nella Chiesa universale* (Rome, 1964).

ROGER AUBERT, born 16 January 1914, in Ixelles-Brussels (Belgium) and ordained in 1938. He studied at the University of Louvain, where he obtained a doctorate in philosophy-history (1933), a doctorate in theology (1942) and further honours (*maîtrise*) in theology (1945). He is also doctor *honoris causa* of the Universities of Nijmegen and Tübingen and the Sacred Heart University in Milan. Since 1952 he has been Professor of Church History at the University of Louvain and is to take over the running of the *Revue d'Histoire Ecclésiastique* and the *Dictionnaire d'Histoire et de Géographie Ecclésiastiques*. His many important published works include *Le Pontificat de Pie IX*, in a new and augmented edition which forms volume XXI of the *Histoire de l'Eglise des origines jusqu'à nos jours* (Paris, 1964) and *Vatican I*, volume XII of the *Histoire des Conciles Oecuméniques* (Paris, 1964).

JOHN COBB, born 9 February 1925, in Kobe (Japan). He is a Methodist and studied in the United States at Emory University (Atlanta) and the University of Chicago. He holds a doctorate in philosophy (1952) and is Professor of Theology at the Theological School in Claremont (California). His published work includes *Living Options in Protestant Theology* (Westminster, 1962) and *The Structure of Christian Existence* (Westminster, 1967).

YVES CONGAR, O.P., born 1904 in Sedan (France) and ordained in 1930. In 1969 he published *L'Ecclésiologie du Haut Moyen Age* and a new edition of *Vraie et fausse réforme dans l'Eglise* (1st edition, 1950). He has edited the section dealing with the period from St Augustine to the present day of the history of ecclesiological doctrines which forms part of the *Dogmengeschichte* published by Herder. In the *Unam Sanctam* series which he founded and which he directs he has brought out detailed commentaries on the texts of Vatican II with the aid of numerous experts. He is a member of the International Theological Commission.

ADELBERT DAVIDS, O.S.B., born 14 May 1937, in Rotterdam (Netherlands). He studied in Louvain, Rome, Salzburg and Munich. He holds a doctorate in theology and is reader in patrology and ancient Church history at the University of Nijmegen.

JACQUES GADILLE, born 6 January 1927, in Choisy le Roi (France). He is a Roman Catholic and studied at Paris. He is *agrégé* in history, holds a doctorate in contemporary history (1967) and is Senior Lecturer at the University of Lyons. His published work includes *Les souvenirs du Vatican d'Albert du Beys 1869-1870* (Louvain, 1968).

LOUIS GOOSEN, born 10 January 1925, in Bergen op Zoom (Netherlands). He is a Roman Catholic and studied at the University of Nijmegen. He is *doctorandus* in theology and is currently preparing his doctoral thesis. He is researching in Church History at the University of Nijmegen.

EUGÈNE HONÉE, born 11 March 1934, in Meerssen (Netherlands). He is a Roman Catholic. He studied at Nijmegen, Rome and Mainz. He is *doctorandus* in theology and is currently preparing his doctoral thesis. He is researching in Church History at the University of Nijmegen.

JAN VAN LAARHOVEN, born 3 August 1926, in Zevenbergschen Hoek (Netherlands). He is a Roman Catholic. He studied at the Gregorian University in Rome. He holds a doctorate in theology and is Professor of Church History at the University of Nijmegen. His published work includes *Een kerkprovincie in concilie* (Utrecht, 1965).

CONRAD W. MÖNNICH, born 31 May 1915, in Amsterdam (Netherlands). He is a member of the Lutheran Evangelical Church and studied at the University of Amsterdam. He holds a doctorate in theology, and since 1943 he has been Professor of Ancient and Medieval Church History in the University of Amsterdam. His published work includes *Geding der vrijheid; de betrekkingen der Oost en West-Kerken tot de val van Constantinopel (1453)* (1967) and *De weg en de wegen, aspecten van de Kerkgeschiedenis* (1959).

BERNARD PLONGERON, born 5 March 1931, in Meaux (France). He was ordained in 1963 and studied at the Sorbonne and at the Theology Faculty in Paris. He holds a licentiate in theology, a higher studies diploma in history and a doctorate in history (1963). He is director of studies at the Catholic Institute in Paris and co-director of the Centre de recherches d'histoire religieuse. His published work includes *Dom Grappin correspondant de l'abbé Grégoire (1796-1830)* (1967).

ANTON WEILER, born 6 November 1927, in Voorburg (Netherlands). He is a Roman Catholic and studied at the University of Nijmegen and at the Ecole des Chartes and the Ecole des Hautes Etudes in Paris. He holds a doctorate in history (1962) and has been Professor of Medieval History, Paleography and Diplomacy at the University of Nijmegen since 1964, where since 1965 he has also taught the philosophy of history. His published work includes *Heinrich von Gorkum. Seine Stellung in der Philosophie und der Theologie des Spätmittelalters* (Hilversum, 1962) and *Nicolaas van Cues en de oecumenische problematiek vóór de Reformatie* (Bois-le-Duc, 1964).